PREFACE

No person on Earth who reads this little work will condemn it : it is only a question how many millions may look through it and benefit them-selves by adopting its precepts.

The Author.

The

BREATH of LIFE

This communication being made in the confident belief that very many of its Readers may draw from it hints of the highest importance to the enjoyment and prolongation of their lives, requires no other apology for its appearance, nor detention of the Reader from the information which it is designed to convey.

With the reading portion of the world it is generally known that I have devoted the greater part of my life in visiting, and recording the looks of, the various native Races of N. & South America; and during those researches, observing the healthy condition and physical perfection of those people, in their primitive state, as contrasted with the deplorable mortality — the numerous diseases and deformities, in civilized communities, I have been led to search for, and able, I believe, to discover, the main causes leading to such different results.

During my Ethnographic labours amongst

those wild people I have visited 150. Tribes, containing more than two millions of souls; and therefore have had, in all probability, more extensive opportunities than any other man living, of examening their sanitary system; and if from those examinations I have arrived at results of importance to the health and existence of mankind, I shall have achieved a double object in a devoted and toilsome life, and shall enjoy a twofold satisfaction in making them known to the world, and particularly to the Medical Faculty, who may perhaps turn them to good account.*

Man is known to be the most perfectly constructed of all the animals, and consequently he can endure more: he can out-travel the Horse — the Dog — the Ox, or any other animal; he can fast longer — his natural life is said to be "3. score and 10. years", while its real, average length, in civilized communities, is but half equal to that of the brutes whose natural term is not one third as long!

This enormous disproportion might be attributed to some natural, physical deficiency in the construction of Man, were it not that we find him in some phases of Savage life, enjoying almost equal exemption from disease and premature death, as the Brute creations; leading us to the irresistible conclusion that there is some lamentable fault yet overlooked in the sanitary economy of civilized life.

The human Race and the various brute —

---

* As the information contained in this little work is believed to be of equal importance to all classes of Society, and of all Nations, the Author has endeavoured to render it in the simplest possible form, free from ambiguity of expression and professional technicality of language that all may be able, alike to appreciate it; and if the

species have alike been created for certain respective terms of existence, and wisely supplied with the physical means of supporting that existence to its intended and natural end; and with the two creations, these powers would alike answer, as intended, for the whole term of natural life, except from some hereditary deficiency, or some practiced abuse.

The horse, the dog, the ox, and others of the brute creations, we are assured by the breeders of those animals, are but little subject to the fatal diseases of the lungs and others of the respiratory or digestive organs; nor to diseases of the spine — to Idiocy or Deafness; and their teeth continuing to perform their intended functions to the close of natural life, not one in a hundred of these animals, with proper care and a sufficiency of food, would fail to reach that period, unless destroyed by intention or accident.

Mankind are everywhere a departure from this sanitary condition, though the Native Races oftentimes present a near approach to it, as I have witnessed amongst the Tribes of North & South Am^a, amongst whom, in their primitive condition, the abovementioned diseases are seldom heard of; and the almost unexceptional regularity, beauty, and soundness of their teeth last them to advanced life and old age.

In civilized communities, better sheltered, less exposed, and with the aid of the ablest professional skill, the sanitary condition of mankind, with its variety, its complication and fatality of diseases —— its aches and pains, & mental &

---

work contains several brief repetitions, they are only those which were intended, and such as always allowed, and even difficult to be avoided, in conveying important advice.

physical deformities, presents a more lamentable and mournful list, which plainly indicates the existence of some extraordinary, latent cause not as yet sufficiently appreciated, and which it is the sole object of this little work to expose.

From the Bills of Mortality which are annually produced in the civilized world, we learn that in London and other large towns in England, and cities of the Continent, on an average, one half of the human Race die before they reach the age of five years, and one half of the remainder die before they reach the age of 25., thus leaving but one in four to share the chances of lasting from the age of 25. to old age.

Statistical accounts showed not many years past, that in London one half of the children died under three years, in Stockholm, one half died under two years, and in Manchester one half died under five years; but owing to recent improved sanitary regulations, the numbers of premature deaths in those cities are much diminished, leaving the average proportions as first given, no doubt, very near the truth, at the present time; and still a lamentable statement for the contemplation of the world, by which is seen the frightful gauntlet that civilized man runs in his passage through life.

The sanitary condition of the Savage Races of North and South America, a few instances of which I shall give, not by quoting a variety of authors, but from estimates carefully made by myself, whilst travelling among those people, will be found to present a striking contrast to those just mentioned, and so widely different as naturally, and very justly, to raise the enquiry into the causes leading to such dissimilar results.

Several very respectable and credible modern writers have undertaken to show, from a host of authors, that premature mortality is greater amongst the Savage, than amongst the Civilized Races; which is by no means true, excepting amongst those communities of savages who have been corrupted, & their simple and temperate modes of life changed by the dissipations and vices introduced among them by civilized people.

In order to draw a fair contrast between the results of habits amongst the two races, it is necessary to contemplate the two people living in the uninvaded habits peculiar to each; and it would be well also, for the writer who draws those contrasts, to see with his own eyes, the customs of the native Races, and obtain his information from the lips of the people themselves, instead of trusting to a long succession of authorities, each of which has quoted from his predecessor, when the original one has been unworthy of credit or has gained his information from unreliable or ignorant, or malicious sources.

There is perhaps, no other subject upon which historians and other writers are more liable to lead the world into erroneous conclusions than that of the true native customs and character of Aboriginal Races; and that from the universal dread and fear which have generally deterred historians and other men of Science from penetrating the solitudes inhabited by these people in the practice of their primitive modes.

There always exists a broad and moving barrier between savage and civilized communities, where the first shaking of hands and acquaintance take place, and over which the demoralizing and deadly effects of dissipation are taught and practiced; and from which, unfortunately, both for the character of the barbarous races and the benefit of science, the customs and the personal appearance of the savage are gathered and portrayed to the world.

It has been too much upon this field that historians & other writers have drawn for the exaggerated accounts which have been published, of the excessive mortality amongst the savage Races of America, leading the world to beleive that the actual premature waste of life caused by the dissipations and vices introduced, with the accompanying changes in the modes of living in such districts, were the proper statistics of those people.

I have visited these semi-civilized degradations of savage life in every degree of latitude in North America, and to a great extent also in Central and South Amª, and as far as this system extends, I agree with those writers who have contended in general terms, that premature mortality is proportionally greater amongst the Native Races than in Civilized communities: but as I have also extended my visits and my enquiries into the tribes in the same latitudes, living in their primitive state — and practicing their native modes, I offer myself as a living witness, that whilst in that condition, the native Races in North and South Amª are a healthier people, and less subject to premature mortality (save from the accidents of War and the Chase, and also from Smallpox and other pestilential diseases introduced amongst them) than any civilized Race in existence.

Amongst a people who preserve no Records and gather no Statistics it has been impossible to obtain exact accounts of their annual deaths, or strict proportionate esti-

-mates of deaths before and between certain ages; but from verbal estimates given me by the Chiefs and Medical men in the various tribes, and whose statements may in general be relied on as very near the truth, there is no doubt but I have been able to obtain information on these points which may safely be relied on as a just average of the premature mortality in many of those Tribes, and which we have a right to beleive would be found to be much the same in most of the others.

As to the melancholy proportions of deaths of children in civilized communities already given, there is certainly no parallel to it to be found amongst the N. or S. Amn. Tribes, where they are living according to their primitive modes; nor do I believe that a similar mortality can be found amongst the children of any aboriginal race on any part of the globe.

Amongst the North Amn. Indians, at all events, where two or three children are generally the utmost results of a marriage, such a rate of mortality could not exist without soon depopulating the country; and as a justification of the general remark I have made, the few following instances of the numerous estimates which I received and recorded amongst the various tribes, I offer in the belief that they will be received as matters for astonishment, calling for some explanation of the causes of so wide a contrast between the Bills of Mortality in the two Races.

Whilst residing in a small village of Guarani of 250. persons, on the banks of the Rio Trombutas, in Brazil; amongst the questions which I put to the Chief, I desired to know as near as possible, the number of children under 10. years of age, which his village had lost within the last 10. years, a space of time over which his recollection could reach with tolerable accuracy. After he and his wife had talked the thing over for some time, they together made the following reply.

viz. — that "they could recollect but three deaths of children within that space of time: one of these was drowned — a second one was killed by the kick of a horse, and the third one was bitten by a Rattle Snake."

This small tribe, or Band, living near the base of the Acarai Mountains, resembled very much in their personal appearance and modes of life, the numerous bands around them; all mounted on good horses; living in a country of great profusion, both of animal and vegetable food

The "Sleepy Eyes." a celebrated chief of a Band of Sioux, in N. Am^{a}., living between the headwaters of the Mississippi and Missouri Rivers, in reply to similar questions, also told me that in his band of 1500. he could not learn from the women that they had lost any of their children in that time, except some two or three who had died from accidents. He told me that the women of his tribe had no instances of Still-born children; and they seemed not even to know the meaning of "Abortions".

I asked him if any of their children were ever known to die from the pains of cutting their teeth, to which he replied, that they always seem to suffer more or less at that period; but that he did not believe that in the whole Sioux Tribe a child ever died from that cause.

(This Tribe I found living in their primitive condition)

Amongst the tribe of Mandans, on the upper Missouri, a tribe of 2000. and living entirely in their primitive state, I learned from the Chiefs, that the death of a child under the age of 10. years was a very unusual occurrence; and from an examination of the dead bodies in their Cemetery, at the back of their village, which were envelloped in skins, and resting separately, on little scaffolds of poles erected on the prairies, amongst some 150. of such I could discover but the embalmments of eleven children, which strongly corroborated in my mind, the statements made to me by the Chiefs, as to the unfre-

-quency of the deaths of children under the age abovementioned; and which I found still further, if not more-strongly, corroborated in the collection of human Skulls preserved and lying on the ground underneath the scaffolds.

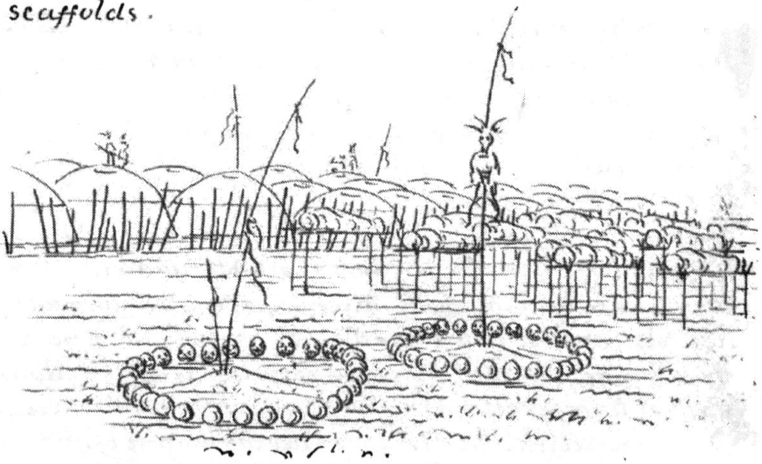

By the custom peculiar to this tribe, when the scaffolds decay, on which the bodies rest, and fall to the ground, the skulls, which are bleached, are carefully and superstitiously preserved in several large circles on the ground; and amongst several hundreds of these skulls, I was forcibly struck with the almost incredibly small proportion of crania of children; and even more so, in the almost unexceptional completeness and soundness (and total absence of malformation) of their beautiful sets of teeth, of all ages, which are scrupulously kept together, by the lower jaws being attached to the other bones of the head. *

---

* A short time after I had described to the World the beautiful formation and polish of the teeth in these Skulls, the forceps came, and (like the most of those left in the Indian graves on the frontiers) - the most beautiful of them, which had chewed Buffalo meat for 25 years or a half Century, are now chewing Bread and Butter, in various parts of the World.

In this Tribe of 2000. I learned also from the chiefs, that there was not an instance of Idiocy or Lunacy – of crooked spine (or hunch back) of Deaf and Dumb, or of other deformity of a disabling kind.

The instances which I have thus far stated, as rather extraordinary cases, of the healthfulness of their children, in the above tribes, are nevertheless, not far different from many others which I have recorded in the numerous tribes which I have visited; and the apparently singular exemption of the Mandans, which I have mentioned, from mental and physical deformities, is by no means peculiar to that tribe; but, almost without exception, is applicable to all the tribes of the Am.^n Continent, where they are living in their primitive condition, and according to their original modes.

(This Tribe subsists chiefly on Buffalo meat, and maize or Indian Corn, which they raised to a considerable extent.)

Amongst two millions of these wild people whom I have visited, I never saw, or heard of a hunch-back (crooked Spine) though my enquiries were made in every tribe: nor did I ever see an Idiot or Lunatic amongst them, though I heard of some three or four, during my travels, and perhaps of as many Deaf and Dumb. *

Shar-re-tar-ruske, an aged and venerable chief of the Pawnee-Picts, a powerful tribe living on the

* Some writers upon whom the world have relied for a correct account of the customs of the Am.^n Indians, have assigned as the cause of the almost entire absence of mental and physical deformities amongst these people, that they are in the habit of putting to death all who are thus afflicted: but such is not only an unfounded and unjust, but disgraceful assumption on the part of those by whom the opinions of the world have been led; for, on the contrary, in every one

head waters of the Arkansas River, at the base of the Rocky Mountains, told me in answer to questions, "we very seldom lose a small child — none of our women have ever died in childbirth — they have no medical attendance on these occasions — we have no idiots or lunatics — nor any Deaf and Dumb, or Hunchbacks, and our children never die in teething."

(This Tribe I found living entirely in their primitive state; their food, Buffalo flesh & Maize, or Indian Corn.

Ski-se-ro-ka — chief of the Kiowas, a small Tribe, on the head waters of the Red River, in western Texas, replied to me — "my wife and I have lost two of our small-children, and perhaps ten or twelve have died in the tribe in the last ten years — — we have lost none of our children by teething — we have no Idiots, no Deaf and Dumb, nor hunchbacks".

(This Tribe I found living in their primitive condition
(their food Buffalo flesh and venison.

Cler-mont. chief of the Osages, replied to my questions, "before my people began to use fire-water, it was a very unusual thing for any of our women to lose their children; but I am sorry to say that we lose a great many of them now. — we have no Fools (Idiots) no Deaf and Dumb, and no hunchbacks — our women never die in childbirth nor have dead children".

---

of the very few cases of the kind, which I have met or could hear of, amongst two millions of these people, these unfortunate creatures were not only supplied and protected with extraordinary care and sympathy, but were in all cases guarded with a superstitious care, as the probable receptacles of some important mystery, designed by the Great Spirit, for the undoubted benefit of the families or Tribes to which they belonged.

Naw-kaw. chief of the Winnebagoes, in Wisconsin, the remnant of a numerous and warlike tribe, now semi-civilized and reduced, "- our children are not now near so healthy as they were - when I was a young man; it was then a very rare thing for a woman to lose her child; now it is a very difficult thing to raise them". - to which his wife added - "since our husbands have taken to drink so much whiskey our babies are not so strong, and the greater portion of them die: we cannot keep them alive." - The chief continued "- we have no Idiots - no Deaf and Dumb, and no hunchbacks - our women never die in childbirth, and they do not allow Doctors to attend them on such occasions."

(food of this tribe, Fish - venison, and vegetables.

Hee-mon-saw - Chief of the Kaskaskias, on the Missouri, once a powerful and warlike tribe, told me that he could recollect when the children of his tribe were very numerous and very healthy, and they had then no Idiots, no deaf & dumb, nor hunchbacks; but that the small-pox and whiskey had killed off the men & women, and the children died very fast. "my Mother", said he, - who is very old, and my little son and myself, all of whom are now before you, are all that are left in my tribe, and I am the chief."!

The above, which are but a very few of the numerous estimates which I have gathered, when compared with the statistics of premature deaths and mental and physical deformities in civilized communities, form a contrast so striking, between the sanitary conditions of the two Races who are born the same, & whose terms of natural life are intended to be equal, as plainly to show, that through the vale of their existence, in civilized Races, there must be some hidden cause of disease not yet sufficiently appreciated, &

which the Materia Medica has not effectually reached.

Under this conviction I have been stimulated to search amongst the Savage Races for the causes of their exemption from, and amongst the civilized communities for the causes of their subjection to, so great a calamity, and this I believe I have discovered, commencing in the cradle, and accompanying civilized mankind through the painful gauntlet of life to the grave; and in possession of this information, when I look into the habits of such communities, and see the operations of this cause, and its lamentable effects, I am not in the least astonished at the frightful results which the lists of mortality show; but it is matter of surprise to me that they are not even more lamentable, and that Nature can successfully battle so long as she does, against the abuses with which she often has to contend.

This cause I believe to be the simple neglect to secure the vital and intended advantages to be derived from quiet and natural sleep; the great physician and restorer of mankind, both Savage and Civil; as well as of the Brute Creations.

Man's cares and fatigues of the day become a daily disease, for which quiet sleep is the cure: And the All-wise Creator has so constructed him that his breathing lungs support him through that sleep, like a perfect machine, regulating the digestion of the stomach & the circulation of the blood, and carrying repose and rest to the utmost extremity of every limb; and for the protection and healthy working of this machine through the hours of repose, He has formed him with nostrils intended for measuring and tempering the air that feeds this moving principle and fountain of life: And in proportion as the quieting and restoring influence of the lungs in natural repose, is carried to every limb and every organ, so in unnatural and abused repose, do they send their complaints to the extremities of the system, in various diseases.

and under continued abuse, fall to pieces themselves, carrying inevitable destruction of the fabric with them in their decay.

The two great and primary phases in life and mutually dependant on each other, are waking & sleeping; and the abuse of either is sure to interfere with the other. For the first of these there needs a lifetime of teaching and practice; but for the enjoyment of the latter, man needs no teaching, provided the regulations of the All-Wise Maker and Teacher can have their way, and are not contravened by pernicious habits or erroneous teaching.

If man's unconscious existence for nearly one third of the hours of his breathing life depends from one moment to another, upon the air that passes through his nostrils, and his repose during those hours, and his bodily health & enjoyment between them, depend upon the soothed and tempered character of the currents that are passed through his nose to his lungs, how mysteriously intricate in its construction and important in its functions, is that feature, and how disastrous may be the omission in education which sanctions a departure from the full and natural use of this wise arrangement?

When I have seen a poor Indian woman in the wilderness, lowering her infant from the breast, and pressing its lips together as it falls asleep in its cradle in the open air, and afterwards looked into the Indian multitude for the results of such a practice, I have said to myself "glorious education! such a Mother deserves to be the nurse of Emperors." And when I have seen the careful, tender mothers in civilized life, covering the faces of their infants sleeping in overheated rooms, with their little mouths open and gasping for breath; and afterwards looked into the multitude, I have been struck with the evident evil and lasting results of this incipient stage of education; & have been more forcibly struck, and shocked, when I have looked into the Bills of Mortality, which I believe to be so frightfully swelled by the results of this habit, thus contracted, and practised in contrvention to Nature's design.

There is no animal in nature excepting Man, that sleeps with the mouth open; and with mankind, I believe the habit, which is not natural, is generally confined to civilized communities, where he is nurtured and raised amidst enervating luxuries and unnatural warmth, where the habit is easily contracted, but carried and practised with great danger to life in different latitudes and different climates; and, in sudden changes of temperature, even in his own house.

The physical conformation of man alone affords sufficient proof that this is a habit against instinct, and that he was made, like the other animals, to sleep with his mouth shut — supplying the lungs with vital air through the nostrils, the natural channels; and a strong corroboration of this fact is to be met with amongst the N. Amn. Indians, who strictly adhere to Nature's law in this respect, and show the beneficial results in their fine and manly forms, and exemption from mental and physical diseases, as has been stated.

The Savage infant, like the offspring of the brute, breathing the natural and wholesome air, generally, from instinct, closes its mouth during its sleep; and in all cases of exception the mother rigidly (and cruelly, if necessary) enforces Nature's Law in the manner explained, until the habit is fixed for life, of the importance of which she seems to be perfectly well aware. But when we turn to civilized life, with all its comforts, its luxuries — its science and its Medical skill, our pity is enlisted for the tender germs of humanity, brought forth and caressed in smothered atmospheres which they can only breathe with their mouths wide open, and nurtured with too much thoughtlessness to prevent their contracting a habit which is to shorten their days with the croup in infancy, or to turn their brains to Idiocy or Lunacy, and their spines to curvatures — or in manhood, their sleep to fatigue and the Nightmare, and

and their lungs and their lives to premature decay. *

If the habit of sleeping with the mouth open is so destructive to the human constitution, and is caused by sleeping in confined and overheated air, and this under the imprudent sanction of Mothers, they become the primary causes of the misery of their own offspring; and to them, chiefly, the world must look for the correction of the error, and, consequently, the benefaction of mankind. They should first be made acquainted with the fact that their infants dont require heated air, and that they had better sleep with their heads out of the window than under their mother's arms. — that middle aged, & old people require more warmth than children, and that to embrace their infants in their arms in their sleep during the night, is to subject them to the heat of their own bodies, — added to that of feather beds and overheated rooms, the relaxing effects of which have been mentioned, with their pitiable and fatal consequences.

There are many, of course, in all ranks and grades of society, who escape from contracting this early and dangerous habit, and others who commence it in childhood, or in manhood, a very few of

---

* The weekly Bills of Mortality in London show an amount of 10. 15. & sometimes 20. deaths of infants per week, from suffocation, in bed with their parents: and Mr. Wakley, in May, 1860. in an inquest on an infant, stated that "he had held inquests over more than 100. Infants which had died during the past winter, from the same cause, their parents covering them entirely over, compelling them to breathe their own breath." (Times)

The Registrar Genl. shows an average of over 700.000. infants born in Engd. per an. and over 100.000. which die under one year of age — 12.738. of these, of Bronchitis. — 3.660. from the pains of teething. and 19.000. of convulsions. — and says — "Suffocation in bed, by overlaying, or shutting off the air from the child, is the most frequent cause of violent deaths of children in England."

whom live and suffer under it to old age, with constitutions sufficiently strong to support Nature in her desperate and continuous struggle against abuse.

When we observe amongst very aged persons that they almost uniformly close the mouth firmly, we are regarding the results of a long practised and healthy habit, and the surviving few who have thereby escaped the fatal consequenses of the evil practice I am condemning.

Though the majority of civilized people are more or less addicted to the habit I am speaking of, comparatively few will admit that they are subject to it. They go to sleep & awake, with their mouths shut, not knowing that the insidious enemy, like the deadly Vampire that imperceptibly sucks the blood, gently steals upon them in their sleep and does its work of death whilst they are unconscious of the evil.

Few people can be convinced that they snore in their sleep, for the snoring is stopped when they awake; and so with breathing through the mouth, which is generally the cause of snoring; — the moment that consciousness arrives the mouth is closed, & Nature resumes her usual course.

In natural and refreshing sleep, man breathes but little air. — his pulse is low; & in the most perfect state of repose he almost ceases to exist. This is necessary, and most wisely ordered, that his lungs, as well as his limbs, may rest from the labour and excitements of the day.

Too much sleep is often said to be destructive to health; but very few persons will sleep too much for their health, provided they sleep in the right way. Unnatural sleep, which is irritating to the lungs and the nervous system, fails to afford that rest which sleep was intended to give, and the longer one lies in it, the less will be the enjoyment and length of his life. Any one waking in the morning at his usual hour of rising, and finding by the dryness of his mouth, that he has been sleeping with the mouth open, feels fatigued, and a wish to go to sleep again; and, convinced that his rest has not been good, he is ready to admit the truth of the statement above made.

There is no perfect sleep for man or brute, with the mouth open; it is unnatural, and a strain upon the lungs which the expression of the countenance and the nervous excitement plainly show.

Lambs, which are nearly as tender as human infants, commence immediately after they are born, to breathe the chilling air of March and April, both night and day, asleep and awake, which they are able to do, because they breathe it in the way that Nature designed them to breathe. New-born infants in the Savage Tribes are exposed to nearly the same necessity, which they endure perfectly well, and there is no reason why the opposite extreme should be practised in the civilized world, entailing so much misfortune and misery on mankind.

It is a pity that at the very <u>starting point</u> of life, — Man should be started wrong — that Mothers should be under the erroneous belief that while their infants are awake they must be watched; but asleep, they are "doing well enough."

Education is twofold, mental and physical; the latter of which alone, at this early stage, can be commenced; and the mother should know that sleep, which is the great renovater and regulator of health, and in fact, the <u>food of life</u>, should be enjoyed in the manner which Nature has designed; and therefore — that her closest scrutiny and watchfulness, like that of the poor Indian woman, should guard her infant in those important hours, when the shooting germs of constitution are starting, on which are to depend the happiness or misery of her offspring.

It requires no more than

common sense to perceive that Mankind, like all the Brute creations, should close their mouths when they close their eyes in sleep, and breathe through their nostrils, which were evidently made for that purpose, instead of dropping the under jaw and drawing an over draught of cold air directly on the lungs, through the mouth; and that in the middle of the night, when the fires have gone down and the air is at its coldest temperature — the system at rest, and the lungs the least able to withstand the shock.

For those who have suffered with weakness of the lungs or other diseases of the chest, there needs no proof of this fact; and for those, if any, who are yet incredulous, it only requires that they should take a candle in their hand and look at their friends asleep and snoring; or with the Nightmare (or without it) with their eyes shut and their mouths wide open, —

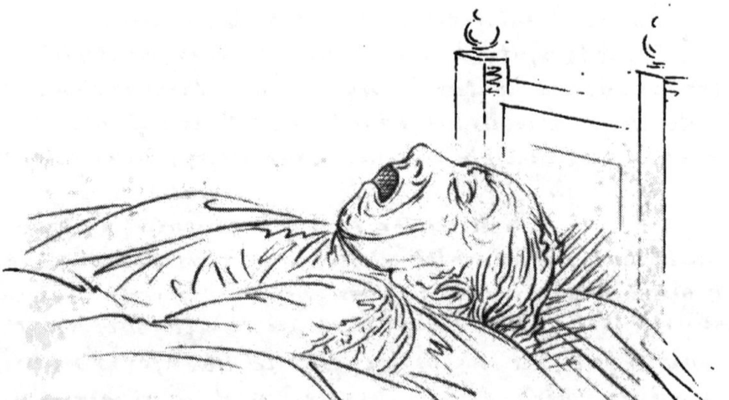

— the very pictures of distress — of suffering, of Idiocy, and Death; when Nature designed that they should be smiling in the soothing and invigourating forgetfulness of the fatigues and anxieties of the day, which —

are dissolving into pleasurable and dreamy shadows of "realities gone bye" ——

Who ever waked out of a fit of the Nightmare in the middle of the night with his mouth strained open & dried to a husk, not knowing when, or from where, the saliva was coming to moisten it again, without being willing to admit the mischief that such a habit might be doing to the lungs, and consequently to the Stomach, the brain, the nerves, and every other organ of the system?

Who, like myself, has suffered from boyhood to middle age, everything but death from this enervating and unnatural habit, and then, by a <u>determined</u> and <u>uncompromising</u> effort, has thrown it off, and gained, as it were, a new lease of life and the enjoyment of rest — which have lasted him to an advanced age through all exposures and privations without admitting the mischief of its consequences?

Nothing is more certain than that for the preservation of human health and life, that most mysterious and incomprehensible, self-acting principle of life which supports us through the restoring and unconscious vale of sleep, should be protected & aided in every way which Nature has prepared for the purpose, and not abused and deranged by forcing the means of its support through a different channel.

We are told that "the breath of life was breathed into man's nostrils" — then why should he not continue to live by breathing it in the same manner? *

The mouth of man, as well as that of the brutes, was made for the reception & mastication of food for the stomach, and other purposes; but the nostrils, with their delicate and fibrous linings for purifying and warming the air in its passage, have been mysteriously constructed, and designed to stand guard over the lungs — to measure the air and equalize its draughts, during the hours of repose.

The atmosphere is nowhere pure enough for man's breathing until it has passed this mysterious refining process; and therefore the imprudence and danger of admitting it in an unnatural way, in double quantities, upon the lungs, and charged with the surrounding epidemic or contagious infections of the moment.

---

* A recently invented aid for the lungs, which the usual efforts for pecuniary results, and the accustomed and unfortunate rage for novelties have been pushing into extensive use, has been doing great mischief in society during the last few years; and by its injudicious use, I believe thousands on thousands have been hurried to the grave. I refer to the "Respirators," so extensively in use, and as generally "in fashion," amongst the Fair Sex. For persons very weak in the lungs, and who have contracted the habit so strong and so long that they cannot breathe excepting through the open mouth, this appliance may be beneficial, in the open air; but thousands of others, to be eccentric or fashionable, place it over their mouths when they step into the street; and to make any use

The impurities of the air which are arrested by the intricate organizations & mucus in the nose are thrown out again from its interiour barriers by the returning breath; and the tingling excitements of the few which pass them, cause the muscular involitions of sneezing, by which they are violently and successfully resisted.

The air which enters the lungs is as different from that which enters the nostrils as distilled water is different from the water in an ordinary cistern or a frog-pond. The arresting and purifying process of the nose, upon the atmosphere with its poisonous igredients, passing through it, though less perceptible, is not less distinct, nor less important than that of the mouth, which stops cherry-stones and fish-bones from entering the stomach.

This intricate organization in the structure of man, unaccountable as it is, seems in a measure divested of mystery, when we find the same phenomena (and others perhaps even more surprising) in the physical conformation of the lower order of animals: and we are again more astonished when we see the mysterious sensitiveness of that organ instinctively and instantaneously separating the gases, as well as arresting and rejecting the material impurities of the atmosphere.

This unaccountable phenomenon is seen in many cases — we see the fish, surrounded with water, breathing the air, upon which it exists. — it is a known fact that man can inhale through his nose, for a certain time, mephetic air, in the bottom of a well, without harm; but if he opens

of it, must open their mouths and breathe through it, by which indiscretion they are thoughtlessly contracting the most dangerous habit which they can subject themselves to, and oftentimes catching their death in a few days, or in a few hours; little aware that closed lips are the best protection against cold air, and their Nostrils the best & safest of all Respirators.

his mouth to answer a question, or calls for help, in that position, his lungs are closed and he expires. Most animals are able to inhale the same for a considerable time without destruction to life, and, no doubt, solely from the fact that their respiration is through the nostrils, in which the poisonous effluvia are arrested.

There are many mineral and vegetable poisons also, which can be inhaled by the nose without harm; but if taken through the mouth destroy life. And so with poisonous reptiles, and poisnous animals. — the man who kills the Rattle snake, or the Copperhead, and stands alone over it, keeps his mouth shut, and receives no harm; but if he has companions with him, with whom he is conversing over the carcases of these reptiles, he inhales the poisonous effluvia through the mouth, & becomes deadly sick, and in some instances death ensues.

Infinitesimal insects also, not visible to the naked eye, are inhabiting every drop of water we drink and every breath of air we breathe; and minute particles of vegetable substances, as well as of poisonous minerals, & even glass and silex, which float imperceptibly in the air, are discovered coating the respiratory organs of man; and the class of birds which catch their food in the air with open mouths as they fly, receive these things in quantities, even in the hollow of their bones, where they are carried and lodged by the currents of air, and detected by microscopic investigation.

Against the approach of these things to the lungs and to the eye, Nature has prepared the guard by the mucous and organic arrangements, calculated to arrest their progress. — Were it not for the liquid in the eye, arresting — neutralizing, and carrying out, the particles of dust communicated through the atmosphere, Man would soon become blind; and but for the mucus in his nostrils, absorbing and carrying off the poisonous particles and effluvia for the protection of the lungs and the brain, mental derangement, consumption of the lungs, and death would ensue.

How easy, and how reasonable, it is to suppose then, that the inhalation of such things to the lungs through the expanded mouth and throat may be a cause of Consumption & the other fatal diseases attaching to the respiratory organs; and how fair a supposition also, that the deaths from the dreadful Epidemics, such as Cholera, Yellow fever, and other pestilences, are caused by the inhalation of animalculae in the infected districts; and that the victims to those diseases are those portions of society who inhale the greatest quantities of those poisonous insects to the lungs and the stomach.

In man's waking hours, when his limbs, and muscles, and his mind, are all in action there may be but little harm in inhaling through the mouth, if he be in a healthy atmosphere; and at moments of violent action and excitement, it may be necessary. But when he lies down at night to rest from the fatigues of the day, and yields his system and all his energies to the repose of sleep; and his volition and all his powers of resistance are giving way to its quieting influence, if he gradually opens his mouth to its widest strain, he lets the enemy in that chills his lungs — that racks his brain — that paralyses his stomach — that gives him the nightmare — brings him Imps and Fairies that dance before him during the night; and during the following day, head-ache — tooth-ache — rheumatism — dispepsia and the gout.

That man knows not the pleasure of sleep; he rises in the morning more fatigued than when he retired to rest — takes pills and remedies through the day, and renews his disease every night. A guilty conscience is even a better guarantee for peaceful rest than such a treatment of the lungs during the hours of sleep. Destructive irritation of the nervous system and inflammation of the lungs, with their consequences, are the immediate results of this unnatural habit; and its continued and more remote effects, consumption of the lungs & death.

Besides this frequent and most fatal of all diseases, Bronchitis — Quinsey — Croup — Asthma & other diseases of the respiratory organs, as well as — Dyspepsia — gout of the stomach — Rickets — Diarrhoea — diseases of the liver, the heart, the spine, & the whole of the nervous system, from the brain to the toes, may chiefly be attributed to this deadly and unnatural habit; and any Physician can easily explain the manner in which these various parts of the system are thus affected by the derangement of the natural functions of the machine that gives them life and motion.

All persons going to — sleep should think, not of their business — not of their riches or poverty — their pains or their pleasures — but, of what are of infinitely greater importance to them, their lungs: their best friends, that have kept them alive through the day and from whose quiet and peaceful repose they are to look for happiness & strength during the toils of the following day. They should first recollect that their natural food is fresh air; and next, that the channels prepared for the supply of that food are the nostrils, which are supplied with the means of purifying the food for the — lungs, as the mouth is constructed to select and masticate the food for the stomach. The lungs should be put to rest as a fond Mother lulls her infant to — sleep; they should be supplied with vital air, and protected in the natural use of it; and for such Care, each successive day would repay in increased pleasures and enjoyments.

The lungs and the stomach are too near neighbours not to be mutually affected by abuses offered to the one or the other. — they both have their natural food, and the —

natural and appropriate means prepared by which it is to be received. Air is the especial food of the lungs, and not of the Stomach. He who sleeps with his mouth open draws cold air and its impurities into the stomach as well as into the lungs; and various diseases of the stomach, with indigestion and dispepsia are the consequences. Bread may almost as well be taken into the lungs, as cold air and wind into the stomach.

A very great proportion of human diseases are attributed to the stomach, and are there met and treated; yet I believe they have a higher origin, the lungs; upon the healthy and regular action of which the digestive, as well as the respiratory and nervous systems depend: the moving, active, principle of life — and — life itself, are there; and whatever deranges the natural action at that fountain affects every — function of the body.

The stomach performs its indispensable, but secondary, part, whilst the moving — motive power is in healthy action, and no longer. Man can exist several days without food, and but about as many minutes, without the action of his lungs. Men habitually say "they dont sleep well, because something is wrong in their stomachs", when the truth may be, that their stomachs are wrong because something is wrong in their sleep.

If this dependent affinity in the human system be true, besetting man's life with so many dangers flowing from the abuse of his lungs, with the fact that the brute creations are exempt from all of these dangers, and the savages in the wilderness nearly so, how important is the question which it raises whether the frightful and unaccountable Bills of Mortality amongst the Civilized Races of Mankind are not greatly augmented, if not chiefly caused, by this error of life, beginning, as I have said, in the cradle, and becoming by habit, as it were, a second nature, to weary and torment Mankind to their graves?

Man is created, we are told, to live — three score and ten years, but how small a proportion of mankind reach that age, or half way, or — even a quarter of the way to it! We learn from the official Reports before alluded to, that in civilized communities, one half or more perish in infancy or childhood, and one half of the remainder between that and the age of 25. and Physicians tell us the dis-diseases they die of; but who tells us of the causes of those diseases? All effects have their causes — disease is the cause of death — and there is a cause for disease.

When we see the Brute creations exempted — from premature death, and the Savage Races comparatively so, whilst Civilized communities show such lamentable Bills of Mortality, it is but a rational deduction that that fatality is the result of habits not practised by Savages and the brute creations; and what other characteristic differences in the habits of the three creations strike us as so distinctly different, and so proportioned to the results, as already shown; the first, with the mouth always shut; the second, with it shut during the night and most of the — day; and the third, with it open most of the day, & all of the night? The first of these are free from disease the second, comparatively so; and the third show the lamentable results in the Bills of Mortality already given.

How forcible and natural is the deduction from these facts, that here may be the great and principal cause of such widely different results, strengthened by the other facts, that the greater part — of the fatal diseases of the body as well as diseases of — the mind, beforementioned, are such as could, and would flow, from such an unnatural abuse of the lungs, the fountain and mainspring of life: and how important also, is the question raised by these facts, — how far such an unnatural habit exposes the human race to the dangers from Epidemic diseases. The Brute creations are everywhere free from the Cholera and Yellow fever, and I am a living witness that the Asiatic Cholera of 1831. was everywhere arrested on the United States frontier, when in its progress it reached the Savage tribes living in — their primitive condition; having been a traveller on those frontiers during its ravages in those regions.

Epidemic diseases are undoubtedly communicated through the medium of the atmosphere, in poisonous animalculae or other infectious agents; and what conclusion can be more rational, than that he who sleeps with his mouth open during the night, drawing an increased quantity of infected atmosphere directly on the lungs and into the stomach will increase his chances of contracting the disease? And how interesting to Science, and how infinitely important to the Welfare of the Human Race might yet be the enquiry, whether the thousands and millions of victims to Cholera and yellowfever, were not those very portions of society who were in the habit of sleeping with their mouths open, in the districts infected with those awful scourges! *

It is a well known fact that fishes will die in a few moments, in their own element, with their mouths kept open by the hook; and I strongly-

---

* My opinions on this important subject having been formed many years ago, as seen in the foregoing pages, I have had opportunities of making observations of an interesting nature, in my recent travels; and amongst those opportunities, one of the most impressive, whilst I was making the voyage on one of the Mail Steamers, from Montevideo to Pernambuco, on the coast of Brazil, in the summer of 1857. during which melancholy voyage about 30. out of 80. passengers died of the Yellow fever, and were launched from the deck into the sea, according to the.

doubt whether a horse or an ox would live any length of time, with its mouth fastened open with a block of wood, during the accustomed hours of its repose; and I believe that the derangement of the system by such an experiment would be similar to that in the human frame, and that death would be sooner and more certain: and I believe also, that if the Amn. Races of Savages which I have visited, had treated this subject with the same indifference and abuse, they would long since have lost (if not have ceased to exist) that decided advantage which they now hold, over the civilized Races, in manly beauty and symmetry of physical conformation: and that their Bills of mortality would exhibit a much nearer approximation to those of the civilized communities than they now do.†

---

custom. Having been twice tried by that disease on former occasions, and consequently feeling little or no alarm for myself, I gave all my time and attention to the assistance of those who were afflicted. Aware of the difficulty of closing the mouth of a corpse whose mouth has been habitually open through life, and observing that nearly every one launched from the vessel had the character and expression strongly impressive of the results of that habit, I was irresistably led to a private and secret scanning of faces at the table and on deck, and of six or seven persons for whom I had consequent apprehensions, I observed their seats were in a day or two vacated, and afterwards I recognized their faces, when brought on deck, as subjects for the last, sad ceremony.

---

† I have before said that the Brute creations are everywhere free from Cholera, Yellow fever, and other epidemics; yet they are as subject as the human Species, to the effects of other poisons. Who knows until it is tried, how long a horse — an ox, or a dog could exist in one of those infected districts, with its mouth fastened open, and its nostrils closed?

how important also,
how far such an unna
to the dangers from E
tions are everywhere fr
and I am a living wit
was everywhere arres
when in its progress it
their primitive cond
frontiers during its

diseases are undou
medium of the atm
or other infectious c
more rational, than
pen during the nig
infected atmosph
stomach will incr
disease? And how
itely important to
yet be the enquir
ions of victims to
very portions of s
with their mouth
those awful sco

fishes will die in
with their mouth

---

* My opinions o
ny years ago, as see
making observati
els; and amongst
whilst I was ma
from Montevi
in the summer
about 30. out
were launched

I have said that no diseases are natural, and deformities, mental and physical, are neither hereditary nor natural, but purely the results of accidents or habits. A cloven-foot produces no cloven-feet, hunch-backs beget straight spines, and mental deformities can have no progeny.

What a sad bill to bring against the glorious advantages of civilized life, its improvements, its comforts and refinements, that in England there are something like 35.000. Idiots and Lunatics — 17.000. Deaf & Dumb & 15.000. hunch-backs, and about an equal proportion of these mental and physical deformities in the other civilized nations of the Earth!

Nature makes nothing without design; and who dares to say that she has designed these lists of pitiable existence amongst the civilized Races of Man, and that the more perfect work of her hand has been bestowed upon the Savage, (and even the Brute) creations? And next to Nature, our dear Mothers, under whose kind care and tender handling we have been raised, could subject us to no accident to turn the brain or crook the spine; but easily & thoughtlessly might, even in their overanxiety for our health, subject us to early treatment, engendering habits which would gradually and imperceptibly produce the whole of these Calamities; which I believe have never as yet, been traced to a more probable cause than the habitual abuse of the lungs, in the manner which has been described.

The teeth of Man, as with the Brutes, are wisely constructed to answer their intended purposes through the natural term of life, and would so, no doubt, but from abuses, the principal one of which I consider to be the pernicious habit already explained. The saliva exuding from the gums, designed as the Element of the teeth, floods every part of the mouth while it is shut; continually rising, like a pure fountain, from the gums, at the —

roots of and between the teeth; loosening and carrying off the extraneous matter which would otherwise accumulate, communicating disease to the teeth, and taint to the breath.

By nature, the teeth and the eyes are strictly amphibious; both immersed in liquids which are prepared for their nourishment and protection, and with powers of existing in the open air long enough for the various purposes for which they were designed; but beyond that, abuse begins, and they soon turn to decay. It is the suppression of saliva, with dryness of the mouth, and an unnatural current of cold air across the teeth and gums during the hours of sleep, that produces malformation of the teeth, toothache, and tic-doloureux, with premature decay, and loss of teeth so lamentably prevalent in the civilized world.

Amongst the Brute creations, that never open their mouths except for taking their food and drink, their teeth are protected from the air both day and night, and seldom decay; but with Man, who is a talking and laughing animal, exposing his teeth to the air a great portion of the day, and oftentimes during the whole of the night, the results are widely different — he is oftentimes toothless at middle age, and in seven cases in ten, in his grave before he is fifty.

If Civilized man, with his usual derangements and absence of teeth, had been compelled to crop the grass, like the ox and the horse, as the means of his living, and knew not the glorious use of the Spoon, to what a misery would he have been doomed, and how long could he exist? the loss of a tooth or two with those animals would result in their death; and how wise, and how provident therefore, the designs of the Creator, who has provided them with the unfailing means of supporting their existence, and also the instinctive habits intended for the protection of those means.

Amongst the Native

Races they seem to have a knowledge of these facts; and the poor Indian woman who watches her infant & presses its lips together as it sleeps in its cradle attracts the ridicule perhaps, or pity, of the passer-bye, but secures the habit in her progeny which enables them to command the admiration and envy of the world.

These people, who talk little and sleep naturally, have no Dentists nor dentifrice, nor do they require either; their teeth almost invariably rise from the gums and arrange themselves as regular as the keys of a piano; and without decay or aches, preserve their soundness and enamel, and powers of mastication, to old age: and there are no sufficient reasons assigned yet, why the same results, or nearly such, may not be produced amongst the more enlightened Races, by similar means.

Civilized man may properly be said to be an open mouthed animal; a wild man is not. An Indian Warrior sleeps, and hunts, and smiles, with his mouth shut; and with seeming reluctance, opens it even to eat or to speak. An Indian child is not allowed to sleep with its mouth open, from the very first sleep of its existence; the consequence of which is, that while the teeth are forming and making their first appearance, they meet (and constantly feel) each other; and taking their relative, natural positions, form that healthful and pleasing regularity which has secured to the Amn. Indians, as a Race, perhaps the most manly and beautiful mouths in the World.*

Nature makes no derangements or deformities in teeth or mouths; but habits or accidents produce the disagreeable derangements of the one, and consequently the disgusting —

* When I speak of comparative personal appearances or of the habits of a people, I speak of them collectively, and in the aggregate. I often see mouths and other physical conformations amongst the Civilized . . .

expressions of the other, which are so often seen.

With the brute creations, where there is less chance for habits or accidents to make derangements, we see the beautiful system of the regularity of the works of Nature's hand, and in their soundness and durability, the completeness of her works, which we have no just cause to beleive has been stinted in the physical construction of Man.

The contrast between the two societies, of Savage and of Civil, as regards the perfection and duration of their teeth, is quite equal to that of their Bills of Mortality, already shown; and I contend that in both cases, the principal cause of the difference is exactly the same, that of respiration through the mouth, during the hours of sleep.

Under the less cruel, and apparently more tender and affectionate treatment, of many civilized —

---

portions of mankind equally beautiful as can be seen amongst the Savage races, but by no means so often. Symmetry of form, gracefulness of movement, and other constituents of manly beauty are much more general amongst the savage Races; & their Societies, free from the humbled and dependent misery which comparative poverty produces in Civilized Communities, produce none of those striking contrasts which stare us in the face, and excite our disgust and our sympathies at nearly every step which we take. The Amⁿ Savages are all poor; their highest want is that of food, which is generally within their reach: their faces are therefore not wrinkled and furrowed with the stamp of care and distress which extreme poverty begets — the repulsive marks which avarice engraves, nor with the loathsome & disgusting expressions which the prodigal dissipations of Wealth often engenders in Civilized societies. Their tastes and their passions are less refined and less ardent, & more seldom excited, & consequently less abused: they live on the simples of life, and imagine and desire only in proportion; the consequences of which are, that their faces exhibit slighter inroads upon Nature, and consequently a greater average of good looks than an equal community of any civilized people.

Mothers, their infants sleep in their arms, in their heated exhalation, or in cradles, in overheated rooms, with their faces covered, without the allowance of a breath of vital air; where, as has been said, they from necessity gasp for breath until it becomes a habit of their infancy and childhood, to sleep with their mouths wide open, which their tender mothers overlook, or are not cruel enough to correct; little thinking of the sad affliction which the croup, or later diseases are to bring into their house.

There is nothing more natural than a mother's near and fond embrace of her infant in her hours of sleep; and nothing more dangerous to its health, and even to its existence. The tender sympathies of love and instinct draw her arms closer around it, and her lips nearer, as she sinks into sleep and compels it to breathe the exhausted and poisoned air that she exhales from her own lungs; little thinking how much she is doing to break her heart in future days. Nothing is sweeter or more harmless to a mother than to inhale the feeble breath of her little innocent; but she should be reminded that whilst she is drawing these delicious draughts, she may be returning for them, pestilence & death.

All mothers know the painful, and even dangerous crisis which their infants pass in teething; and how naturally do their bosoms yearn for the sufferings of these little creatures whose Earthly careers are often stopped by that event. (3.660. per an. in Engd. alone, under one year of age, as has been shown)

Amongst the Savage Races, we have seen, that death seldom, if ever, ensues from this cause; and how easy it is to perceive that unnatural pains, and even death, may be caused by the habit of infants sleeping with their mouths strained open, and exposed to the cold air, when the germs of the teeth are first making their appearance.

The Statistics of England show an annual re-

-turn of "25.000. infants, and children under five years of age that die of Convulsions". —— what causes so probable for those convulsions as teething and the Croup; and what more probable cause for the unnatural pains of teething & the Croup, than the infernal habit which I am condemning.

At this tender age, and under the kind treatment just mentioned, is thoughtlessly laid the foundation for the rich harvests which the Dentists are reaping in most parts of the civilized world. The infant passes two thirds of its time in sleep, with its mouth open, while the teeth are presenting themselves in their tender state, to be chilled and dried in the currents of air passing over them, instead of being nurtured by the warmth and saliva intended for their protection, when they project to unnatural and unequal lengths, or take different and unnatural directions, producing those disagreeable and unfortunate combinations —— ——

—— which are frequently seen in civilized adult societies, and oftentimes sadly disfiguring the human face for life.

While there are a great many persons in all civilized societies who adhere to the designs of Nature in the habits above referred to, how great a proportion of the individuals of those societies carry on their faces the proofs of a different habit, brought from their childhood, — which their Constitutions have so far successfully battled against, until, (as has been said) it becomes like a second Nature, and a matter of necessity, even during their waking — hours and the usual avocations of life, to breathe through the mouth, which is constantly open; while the nasal ducts, being vacated, like vacated roads that grow up to grass & weeds, become the seat of Polypus and other diseases.

In all of these instances there is a derangement and deformity of the teeth, and disfigurment of the mouth, and the whole face, which are not natural; carrying the proof of a — long practice of the baneful habit, with its lasting consequences; and producing that unfortunate & pitiable, and oftentimes disgusting, expression, which none but Civilized communities can present. ——

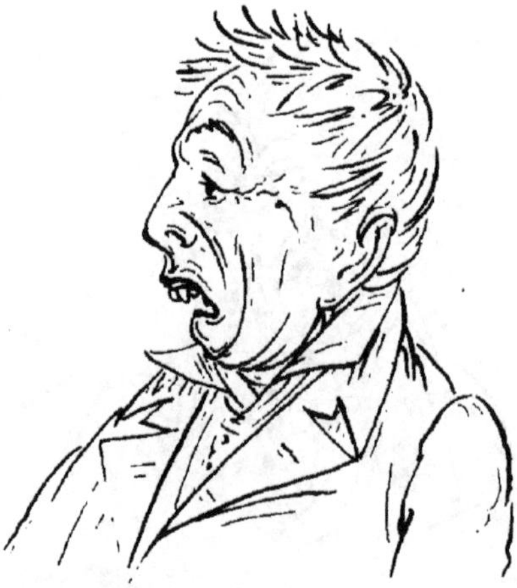

Even the Brute creations furnish nothing so abominable as these; which justly demand our sympathy instead of our derision. The faces and the mouths of the Wolf — the Tiger, and even the Hyena and the Donkey, are agreeable, and even handsome, by the side of them.

What Physician —

how important also, is the question raised by these facts,— how far such an unnatural habit exposes the human race to the dangers from Epidemic diseases. The Brute creations are everywhere free from the Cholera and Yellow fever, and I am a living witness that the Asiatic Cholera of 1831. was everywhere arrested on the United States frontier, when in its progress it reached the Savage tribes living in their primitive condition; having been a traveller on those frontiers during its ravages in those regions.

Epidemic diseases are undoubtedly communicated through the medium of the atmosphere, in poisonous animalculae or other infectious agents; and what conclusion can be more rational, than that he who sleeps with his mouth open during the night, drawing an increased quantity of infected atmosphere directly on the lungs and into the stomach will increase his chances of contracting the disease? And how interesting to Science, and how infinitely important to the Welfare of the Human Race might yet be the enquiry, whether the thousands and millions of victims to Cholera and yellow fever, were not those very portions of society who were in the habit of sleeping with their mouths open, in the districts infected with those awful scourges! *

It is a well known fact that fishes will die in a few moments, in their own element, with their mouths kept open by the hook; and I strongly-

---

* My opinions on this important subject having been formed many years ago, as seen in the foregoing pages, I have had opportunities of making observations of an interesting nature, in my recent travels; and amongst those opportunities, one of the most impressive, whilst I was making the voyage on one of the Mail Steamers, from Montevideo to Pernambuco, on the coast of Brazil, in the summer of 1857. during which melancholy voyage about 30. out of 80. passengers died of the Yellow fever, and were launched from the deck into the sea, according to the-

doubt whether a horse or an ox would live any length of time, with its mouth fastened open with a block of wood, during the accustomed hours of its repose; and I believe that the derangement of the system by such an experiment would be similar to that in the human frame, and that death would be sooner and more certain: and I believe also, that if the Amn. Races of Savages which I have visited, had treated this subject with the same indifference and abuse, they would long since have lost (if not have ceased to exist) that decided advantage which they now hold, over the civilized Races, in manly beauty and symmetry of physical conformation: and that their Bills of mortality would exhibit a much nearer approximation to those of the civilized communities than they now do.†

---

custom. Having been twice tried by that disease on former occasions, and consequently feeling little or no alarm for myself, I gave all my time and attention to the assistance of those who were afflicted. Aware of the difficulty of closing the mouth of a corpse whose mouth has been habitually open through life, and observing that nearly every one launched from the vessel had the character and expression strongly impressive of the results of that habit, I was irresistably led to a private and secret scanning of faces at the table and on deck, and of six or seven persons for whom I had consequent apprehensions, I observed their seats were in a day or two vacated, and afterwards I recognized their faces, when brought on deck, as subjects for the last, sad ceremony.

---

† I have before said that the Brute creations are everywhere free from Cholera, Yellow fever, and other epidemics; yet they are as subject as the human Species, to the effects of other poisons. Who knows until it is tried, how long a horse — an ox, or a dog could exist in one of those infected districts, with its mouth fastened open, and its nostrils closed?

Besides the list of fatal diseases already given, & which I attribute chiefly to the pernicious habit which I have explained, there are other results affecting the senses, personal appearance, and the enjoyments of life, which, though not fatal, are themselves of sufficient importance to demand its correction; such as — Curvature of the Spine — Idiocy — Deafness — Night-mare — Polypus in the Nose — Malformation and premature decay of the teeth — toothache — tic-doloureux — Rheumatism — Gout, and many others to which the brute creations are strangers, and to most of which the Savage Races are but little subject.

By another reference to the Statistics of civilized Societies, we find that in some, — one half per-cent are Idiots or Lunatics: 1/3 pr. ct. are Deaf & Dumb, — 1/2 per cent are hunch-backs, and from 3/4 to 1. per ct. of other disabling diseases and deformities; all of which are almost unknown to the Amn. Native Races; affording a strong corroborative proof, if it were necessary, that such deficiencies and deformities are the results of accidents or habits, and not the works of Nature's hand.

Nature produces no diseases, nor deformities; but the offsprings of men and women whose systems are impaired by the habits which have been alluded to, are no doubt oftentimes ushered into the world with constitutional weaknesses and predilections for contracting the same habits, with their results; and it is safe to say, that three fourths of the generating portions of every civilized community existing, are more or less under these disqualifications, — which, together with want of proper care of their offspring, in infancy and childhood, I believe to be the cause four-fifths of the mental and physical deformities, loss of teeth, and premature deaths, between conception and infancy — childhood — manhood, and old age.

I have said that no diseases are natural, and deformities, mental and physical, are neither hereditary, nor natural, but purely the results of accidents or habits. A cloven-foot produces no cloven-feet, hunch-backs beget straight spines, and mental deformities can have no progeny.

What a sad bill to bring against the glorious advantages of civilized life, its improvements, its comforts and refinements, that in England there are something like 35.000. Idiots and Lunatics — 17.000. Deaf & Dumb & 15.000. hunch-backs, and about an equal proportion of these mental and physical deformities in the other civilized nations of the Earth!

Nature makes nothing without design: and who dares to say that she has designed these lists of pitiable existence amongst the civilized Races of Man, and that the more perfect work of her hand has been bestowed upon the Savage, (and even the Brute) creations? And next to Nature, our dear Mothers, under whose kind care and tender handling we have been raised, could subject us to no accident to turn the brain or crook the spine; but easily & thoughtlessly might, even in their overanxiety for our health, subject us to early treatment, engendering habits which would gradually and imperceptibly produce the whole of these Calamities; which I believe have never as yet, been traced to a more probable cause than the habitual abuse of th lungs, in the manner which has been described.

The teeth of Man, as with the Brutes, are wisely constructed to answer their intended purposes through the natural terme of life, and would so, no doubt, but from abuses, the principal one of which I consider to be the pernicious habit already explained. The saliva exuding from the gums, designed as the Element of the teeth, floods every part of the mouth while it is shut; continually rising, like a pure fountain, from the gums, at the —

roots of and between the teeth; loosening and carrying off the extraneous matter which would otherwise accumulate, communicating disease to the teeth, and taint to the breath.

By nature, the teeth and the eyes are strictly amphibious; both immersed in liquids which are prepared for their nourishment and protection, and with powers of existing in the open air long enough for the various purposes for which they were designed; but beyond that, abuse begins, and they soon turn to decay. It is the suppression of saliva, with dryness of the mouth, and an unnatural current of cold air across the teeth and gums during the hours of sleep, that produces malformation of the teeth, toothache, and tic-douloureux, with premature decay, and loss of teeth so lamentably prevalent in the civilized world.

Amongst the Brute creations, that never open their mouths except for taking their food and drink, their teeth are protected from the air both day and night, and seldom decay; but with Man, who is a talking and laughing animal, exposing his teeth to the air a great portion of the day, and oftentimes during the whole of the night, the results are widely different — he is oftentimes toothless at middle age, and in seven cases in ten, in his grave before he is fifty.

If Civilized man, with his usual derangements and absence of teeth, had been compelled to crop the grass, like the ox and the horse, as the means of his living, and knew not the glorious use of the Spoon, to what a misery would he have been doomed, and how long could he exist? the loss of a tooth or two with those animals would result in their death; and how wise, and how provident therefore, the designs of the Creator, who has provided them with the unfailing means of supporting their existence, and also the instinctive habits intended for the protection of those means.

Amongst the Native

Races they seem to have a knowledge of these facts; and the poor Indian woman who watches her infant & presses its lips together as it sleeps in its cradle attracts the ridicule perhaps, or pity, of the passer-bye, but secures the habit in her progeny which enables them to command the admiration and envy of the world.

These people, who talk little and sleep naturally, have no Dentists nor dentifrice, nor do they require either; their teeth almost invariably rise from the gums and arrange themselves as regular as the keys of a piano; and without decay or aches, preserve their soundness and enamel, and powers of mastication, to old age: and there are no sufficient reasons assigned yet, why the same results, or nearly such, may not be produced amongst the more enlightened Races, by similar means.

Civilized man may properly be said to be an <u>open mouthed animal</u>; a wild man is not. An Indian Warrior sleeps, and hunts, and smiles, with his mouth shut; and with seeming reluctance, opens it even to eat or to speak. An Indian child is not allowed to sleep with its mouth open, from the very first sleep of its existence; the consequence of which is, that while the teeth are forming and making their first appearance, they <u>meet</u> (and constantly <u>feel</u>) each other; and taking their relative, natural positions, form that healthful and pleasing regularity which has secured to the Amn. Indians, as a Race, perhaps the most manly and beautiful mouths in the World.*

Nature makes no derangements or deformities in teeth or mouths; but habits or accidents produce the disagreeable derangements of the one, and consequently the disgusting –

---

* When I speak of comparative personal appearance or of the habits of a people, I speak of them collectively, and in the aggregate. I often see mouths and other physical conformations amongst the Civilized . . .

expressions of the other, which are so often seen.

With the brute creations, where there is less chance for habits or accidents to make derangements, we see the beautiful system of the regularity of the works of Nature's hand, and in their soundness and durability, the completeness of her works, which we have no just cause to beleive has been stinted in the physical construction of Man.

The contrast between the two societies, of Savage and of Civil, as regards the perfection and duration of their teeth, is quite equal to that of their Bills of Mortality, already shown; and I contend that in both cases, the principal cause of the difference is exactly the same, that of respiration through the mouth, during the hours of sleep.

Under the less cruel, and apparently more tender and affectionate treatment, of many civilized —

---

portions of mankind equally beautiful as can be seen amongst the Savage races, but by no means so often. Symmetry of form, gracefulness of movement, and other constituents of manly beauty are much more general amongst the savage Races, & their Societies, free from the humbled and dependent misery which comparative poverty produces in Civilized Communities, produce none of those striking contrasts which stare us in the face, and excite our disgust and our sympathies at nearly every step which we take. The Amn. Savages are all poor; their highest want is that of food, which is generally within their reach: their faces are therefore not wrinkled and furrowed with the stamp of care and distress which extreme poverty begets — the repulsive marks which avarice engraves, nor with the loathsome & disgusting expressions which the prodigal dissipations of Wealth often engenders in Civilized societies. Their tastes and their passions are less refined and less ardent, & more seldom excited, & consequently less abused: they live on the simples of life, and imagine and desire only in proportion; the consequences of which are, that their faces exhibit — slighter inroads upon Nature, and consequently a greater average of good looks than an equal community of any civilized people.

Mothers, their infants sleep in their arms, in their heated exhalation, or in cradles, in overheated rooms, with their faces covered, without the allowance of a breath of vital air; where, as has been said, they from necessity gasp for breath until it becomes a habit of their infancy and childhood, to sleep with their mouths wide open, which their tender mothers overlook, or are not cruel enough to correct; little thinking of the sad affliction which the croup, or later diseases are to bring into their house.

There is nothing more natural than a mother's near and fond embrace of her infant in her hours of sleep; and nothing more dangerous to its health, and even to its existence. The tender sympathies of love and instinct draw her arms closer around it, and her lips nearer, as she sinks into sleep and compels it to breathe the exhausted and poisoned air that she exhales from her own lungs; little thinking how much she is doing to break her heart in future days. Nothing is sweeter or more harmless to a mother than to inhale the feeble breath of her little innocent; but she should be reminded that whilst she is drawing these delicious draughts, she may be returning for them, pestilence & death.

All mothers know the painful, and even dangerous crisis which their infants pass in teething; and how naturally do their bosoms yearn for the sufferings of these little creatures whose Earthly careers are often stopped by that event. (3.660. per an. in Engd. alone, under one year of age, as has been shown)

Amongst the Savage Races, we have seen that death seldom, if ever, ensues from this cause; and how easy it is to perceive that unnatural pains, and even death, may be caused by the habit of infants sleeping with their mouths strained open, and exposed to the cold air, when the germs of the teeth are first making their appearance.

The Statistics of England show an annual re-

-turn of "25.000. infants, and children under five years of age that die of Convulsions". —— what causes so probable for those convulsions as teething and the Croup; and what more probable cause for the unnatural pains of teething & the Croup, than the infernal habit which I am condemning.

At this tender age, and under the kind treatment just mentioned, is thoughtlessly laid the foundation for the rich harvests which the Dentists are reaping in most parts of the civilized world. The infant passes two thirds of its time in sleep, with its mouth open, while the teeth are presenting themselves in their tender state, to be chilled and dried in the currents of air passing over them, instead of being nurtured by the warmth and saliva intended for their protection, when they project to unnatural and unequal lengths, or take different and unnatural directions, producing those disagreeable and unfortunate combinations ——

—— which are frequently seen in civilized adult societies, and oftentimes sadly disfiguring the human face for life.

While there are a great many persons in all civilized societies who adhere to the designs of Nature in the habits above referred to, how great a proportion of the individuals of those societies carry on their faces the proofs of a different habit, brought from their childhood,—which their Constitutions have so far successfully battled against, until, (as has been said) it becomes like a second Nature, and a matter of necessity, even during their waking—hours and the usual avocations of life, to breathe through the mouth, which is constantly open; while the nasal ducts, being vacated, like vacated roads that grow up to grass & weeds, become the seat of Polypus and other diseases.

In all of these instances there is a derangement and deformity of the teeth, and disfigurment of the mouth, and the whole face, which are not natural; carrying the proof of a—long practice of the baneful habit, with its lasting consequences; and producing that unfortunate & pitiable, and oftentimes disgusting, expression, which none but Civilized communities can present. ——

Even the Brute creations furnish nothing so abominable as these; which justly demand our sympathy instead of our derision. The faces and the mouths of the Wolf—the Tiger, and even the Hyena and the Donkey, are agreeable, and even handsome, by the side of them.

What Physician—

will say that the inhalation of cold air to the lungs through such mouths as these, and over the putrid secretions and rotten teeth within, may not occasion disease of the lungs and death? Infected districts communicate disease — infection attaches to putrescence, and no other infected district can be so near to the lungs as an infected mouth.

Most habits against Nature, if not arrested, run into disease. The habit which has thus far been treated as a habit, merely, with its evil consequences, will here be seen to be worthy of a name, and of being ranked amongst the specific diseases of mankind; Indulged and practised until the mouth is permanently distorted from its natural shape, and in the infectious state above named, acting the unnatural hand-maid to the lungs, it gains the locality and speciality of character which characterize diseases, and therefore would properly rank amongst them. No name seems as yet to have been applied to this malady, and no one apparently more expressive, at present suggests, than Malo inferno, which (though perhaps not exactly Classic) I would denominate it, and define it to be — strictly a human disease — confined chiefly to the Civilized Races of Man. — an unnatural and pitiable disfigurement of the "human face divine," unknown to the Brutes, and unallowed by the Savage Races — Caused by the careless permission of a habit contracted in infancy or childhood, and submitted to, humbly, through life, under the mistaken belief that it is by an unfortunate order of Nature — its Remedy. (in neglect of the specifics to be proposed in the following pages) the grave, (generally) between infancy and the age of forty.

The Amn. Indians call the civilized Races "pale faces" and "black mouths", and to understand the full force of these expressions, it is necessary to live awhile amongst the Savage Races, and then to return to civilized life. The Author has had ample opportunities of testing the justness of these expressions, and has been forcibly struck with the correetness of their application, on returning from Savage to civilized Society. A long familiarity with red-faces and closed mouths affords a new view of our friends when we get back, and fully explains to us the horror which a savage has of a "pale-face", and his disgust with the expression of open & black mouths. *

No man or woman with a handsome set of teeth keeps the mouth habitually open; and every person with an unnatural derangement of the teeth is as sure, seldom to have it shut. This is not because the derangement of the teeth has made the habit, but because the habit has caused the derangement of the teeth.

If it were for the sake of the teeth alone, and man's personal appearance, the habit I am condemning would be one well worth struggling against; but when we can so easily, & with so much certainty discover its destructive effects upon the constitition and life of man, it becomes a subject of a different importance, and well worthy of being understood by every member of society, who themselves, and not physicians, are to arrest its deadly effects.

The Brute, at its birth, rises on its feet — breathes the open air, & seeks and obtains its food at the next moment. The Chicken breaks its own shell and walks out on two —

---

* Of the party of 14. Ioway Indians who visited London some years since, there was one whose name was Wash-ke-mon-ye (the fast dancer) he was a great droll, and somewhat of a critic; and had picked up enough of English to enable him to make a few simple sentences and to draw amusing comparisons. I asked him one day, how he liked the White people, after the experience he had now had; to which he replied — "well — white man — suppose — mouth shut, pretty good — mouth

legs, and without a gaze of wonder upon the world around, begins selecting and picking up its own food!

Man, at his birth, is a more helpless animal, and his mental, as well as his physical faculties, requiring a much longer time to mature, are subject to greater dangers of misdirection from pernicious habits, which it should be the first object of parents to guard against.

The Savage Tribes of Am^n^ allow no obstacles to the progress of Nature in the developement of their teeth and their lungs for the purposes of life, and consequently securing their exemption from many of the pangs and pains which the civilized Races seem to be heirs to; who undoubtedly too often over-educate the intellect, while they under-educate the... Man.

The human infant, like the infant brute, is able to breathe the natural air at its birth, both asleep and awake; — but that breathing should be done as Nature designed it, through the nostrils, instead of through the mouth.

The Savage Mother, instead of embracing her infant in her sleeping hours, in the heated exhalation of her body, places it at her arm's length from her, and compels it to breathe the fresh air, the coldness of which generally prompts it to shut the mouth, in default of which, she presses its lips together in the manner that has been stated, until she fixes the habit which is to last it through life; and the contrast to this, which is too often practiced by mothers in the civilized world, in the mistaken belief that warmth is the essential thing for their darling babes, I believe to be the inno—

---

open, no coot — me no like um, not much". This reply created a smile amongst the party, and the chief informed me that one of the most striking peculiarities which all Indian Tribes discovered amongst the white people, was the derangement & absence of their teeth, & which they believed were destroyed by the number of lies that passed over them.

—cent foundation for the principal, and as yet unex plained cause of the deadly diseases so frightfully — swelling the Bills of Mortality in civilized communities.

All Savage infants amongst the various native Tribes of America, are reared in cribs (or Cradles)

— with the back lashed to a straight board; and by the aid of a circular, concave cushion placed uder the — head, the head is bowed a little forward when they — sleep, which prevents the mouth from falling open; thus establishing the early habit of breathing through the nostrils. The results of this habit are, that Indian adults invariably walk erect and straight — have healthy spines, and sleep upon their backs —

— with their Robes wrapped around them; with the head supported by some rest, which inclines it a little forward — or upon their faces, with the forehead resting on the arms which are folded underneath it. —— —

—— in both of which cases there is a tendency to the closing of the mouth; and their sleep is therefore always unattended with the Nightmare or snoring.

Lying on the back is thought by many to be an unhealthy practice; and a long habit of sleeping in a different position may even make it so: but the general custom of the Savage races, of sleeping in this position from infancy to old age, affords very conclusive proof, that if commenced in early life, it is the healthiest for a general posture, that can be adopted.

It is very evident that the back of the head should never be allowed, in sleep, to fall to a level with the spine; but should be supported by a small pillow, to elevate it a little, without raising the shoulders or bending the back, which should always be kept straight.

The Savages with their pillows, like the birds in the building of their nests, make no improvements during the lapse of ages, and seem to care little if they are blocks of wood or of stone, provided they elevate the head to the required position.

With the civilized Races ——

where everything is progressive, and luxuries especially so, pillows have increased in longitudinal dimensions until they too often form a support for the shoulders as well as the head, thereby annuling the object for which they were originally intended, and for which, alone, they should be used.

All animals — lower the head in sleep; and mankind, with a small support under it, inclining it a little forward, assume for it a similar position.

This elderly and excellent — Gentleman — —

— —from a long (and therefore necessary) habit, takes his nap after dinner, in the attitude which he is contented to believe is the most luxurious that can — be devised; whilst any one can discover that he is very far from the actual enjoyment which he might feel, and the more agreeableness of aspect which he might present to his surrounding friends, if his invention had carried him a little farther, and suggested the introduction of a small cushion behind his head, advancing it a little forward, above the —

level of his spine. The gastric juices commence their work upon the fresh contents of a stomach, on the arrival of a good dinner, with a much slighter jar upon the digestive and nervous systems, when the soothing & delectable compound is not shocked by the unwelcome inhalations of chilling atmosphere.

And this tender and affectionate Mother, blessing herself and her flock of little ones with the pleasures of Sleep!

—— – how much might she increase her own enjoyment with her pillow under her head, instead of having it under her shoulders; and that of her little gasping innocents, if she had placed them in cribs, & with pillows under their heads, from which they could not escape — —.

The contrast between the expressions of these two groups

will be striking to all; and every mother may find a lesson in them worth her studying; either for improvements in her own Nursery, or for teaching those who may stand more in need of Nursery Reform than her self.

So far back as the starting point in life, I believe man seldom looks for the causes of the pangs and pains which beset and torture him in advanced life; but in which, far back as it may be, they may have had their origin.

Little does he think that his aching, deformed, and decaying teeth were tortured out of their natural arrangement and health, in the days of their formation, by the cold draughts of air across them: or that the consumption of his decaying lungs has been caused by the same habit; and that habit was the result of the actual tenderness, but oversight, of his affectionate Mother, when he slept in her arms, or in the cradle.

The foregoing are general remarks which I have been enabled to make, from long and careful observation; and there are others perhaps, equally or more demonstrative of the danger of the habit alluded to, as well as of the power we have of averting it — and of arresting its baneful effects, even in middle age, or the latter part of man's life, which will be found in the relation of my own experience.

At the age of 34. years, (after devoting myself to the dry and tedious study of the Law for 3. years, and to the practice of it for 3. years more — and after that to the still more fatiguing and confining practice of Miniature and portrait painting, for 8. years,) I penetrated the vast wilderness with my canvass and brushes, for the purpose which has already been explained; and in the prosecution of which design, I have devoted most of the subsequent part of my life.

At that period I was exceedingly feeble, which I attributed to the sedentary habits of my occupation, – but which many of my friends and my Physician believed to be the result of disease of the lungs. I had however, no apprehensions that dampened in the least, the ardour and confidence with which I entered upon my new ambition, which I pursued with enthusiasm and unalloyed satisfaction until my researches brought me into solitudes so remote that beds, and bed chambers with fixed air, became matters of impossibility, and I was brought to the absolute necessity of sleeping in canoes or hammocks, or upon the banks of the Rivers, between a couple of Buffalo skins, spread upon the grass, and breathing the chilly air of dewy and foggy nights, – that was circulating around me.

Then commenced a – a struggle of no ordinary kind, between the fixed determination I had made, to accomplish my new ambition, and the daily and hourly pains I was suffering, & the discouraging weakness daily increasing on me, and threatening my ultimate defeat.

I had been, like too many of the world, too tenderly caressed in my infancy and childhood, by the over kindness of an affectionate Mother, without cruelty or thoughtfulness enough to compel me to close my mouth in my sleeping hours; and who, through my boyhood, thinking that while I was asleep I was "doing well enough", allowed me to grow up, under – that abominable custom of sleeping, much of the time, with the mouth wide open; and which practice I thoughtlessly carried into manhood, with Nightmare and snoring, and its other results; and at last, (as I discovered just in time to save my life,) to the banks of the Missouri, where I was nightly drawing the deadly draughts of – cold air, with all its poisonous malaria, through my mouth into my lungs.

Waking many times during

the night, and finding myself in this painful condition, and suffering during the succeeding day with pain and inflammation (and sometimes bleeding) of the lungs, I became fully convinced of the danger of the habit, and resolved to overcome it, which I eventually did, only by sternness of resolution and perseverance; determining through the day, to keep my teeth and my lips firmly closed, except when it was necessary to open them; and strengthening this determination, as a matter of life or death, at the last moment of consciousness, while entering into sleep.

Under this unyielding determination, and the evident relief I began to feel from a partial correction of the habit, I was encouraged to continue in the unrelaxed application of my remedy, until I at length completely conquered an insidious enemy that was nightly attacking me in my helpless position, and evidently fast hurrying me to the grave.

Convinced of the danger I had averted by my own perseverance, and gaining strength for the continuance of my daily fatigues, I renewed my determinations to enjoy my natural respiration during my hours of sleep, which I afterwards did, without difficulty, in all latitudes, in the open air, during my subsequent years of exposure in the wilderness; and have since done so to the present time of my life; when I find myself stronger, & freer from aches and pains than I was from my boyhood to middle age, and in all respects enjoying better health than I did during that period.

I mention these facts for the benefit of my fellow beings, of whom there are tens, (and hundreds) of thousands suffering from day to day from the ravages of this insidious enemy that preys upon their lungs in their unconscious moments, who know not the cause of their sufferings, and find not the Physician who can cure them.

Finding myself so evidently relieved from the —

painful and alarming results of a habit which I recollected to have been brought from my boyhood, I became forcibly struck with the custom I had often observed (and to which I have before alluded) of the Indian women pressing together the lips of their sleeping infants, for which I could not, at first, imagine the motive, but which was now suggested to me in a manner which I could not misunderstand; and appealing to them for the object of so, apparently, cruel a mode, I was soon made to understand, both by their women and their Medicine Men, that it was done "to ensure their good looks, and prolong their lives"; and by looking into their communities, and contrasting their sanitary condition with the Bills of Mortality amongst the Civilized Races, I am ready to admit the justness of their reply; and am fully convinced of the advantages those ignorant Races have over us in this respect, not from being ahead of us, but from being behind us, and consequently not so far departed from Nature's wise and provident regulations, as to lose the benefit of them.

From the whole amount of observations I have made amongst the two classes of society, added to my own experience, as explained in the foregoing pages, I am compelled to beleive, and feel authorised to assert, that a great proportion of the diseases prematurely fatal to human life; as well as mental and physical deformities, and destruction of the teeth; are caused by the abuse of the lungs, in the Mal-respiration of Sleep: and also, that the pernicious habit, though contracted in infancy or childhood, or manhood, may generally be corrected by a steady and determined perseverance, based upon a conviction of its baneful and fatal results.

The great error is most frequently committed, & there is the proper place to correct or prevent it, at the starting point — when the germs are tender, & taking their first impressions, which are to last them —

through life. It is then too, that the fondest and tenderest sympathies belonging to the human breast are watching over them; and it is only necessary for those kind guardians to be made aware of the danger of thoughtless habits which their over-indulgence may allow their offspring to fall into.

It is to Mothers, and truly not to Physicians or Medicines, that the world are to-look, for the remedy of this evil; and the physical improvements of mankind, and the prolongation of human-existence, effected by it.

Children, I have said, are not born Hunchbacks, but a habit of sleeping thus — —

— – in the varying temperatures of the night, might – make them such. Infants are not born Idiots or Lunatics. but a habit of sleeping thus,

— —— in sudden changes of weather, would-tend to make them so. – – — — —— ——

—— —— — and in the countries where infants sleep thus ——

—— the above deformities scarcely exist; while in England, as has been shown, there are 20.000. of the first of these, & 35.000. of the latter. How significant and important the deductions from these simple facts, — if they be facts — and who will contradict them?

If Physicians and Surgeons gain fame for occasionally conquering the enemy in combat; what laurels, and what new Title, should await the fair Diplomatists who will keep the enemy out of the field — the affectionate mothers, who, like the Indian woman, will sit by their sleeping infants, and watch and guard them through their childhood, against the departure from one of Nature's most wise and important regulations, designed for their health and happiness.

If the great majority of this sort of evil has its origin in that early period of life, its correction comes directly under the Mother's province; and there certainly can be no better guarantee for the benefit of coming generations, than that mothers should be made fully sensible of the evil, and of their own power to avert it. And to Mothers, I would in the first place — say —— for the sakes of your infants unborn, and for your own lives sake, draw the curtain, (not of your bed, but of your lungs) when you retire to rest; availing yourselves and your offspring of the full benefit of the peaceful and invigourating repose which Nature has prepared for you, to enable you to meet with success the events to which you are approaching; and when Nature has placed in your arms for your kind care, the darling objects of your tenderest affections, not to forget that she has prepared and designed them to breathe the open air; and that when they sleep in your embrace in heated rooms and feather beds, they sleep in a double or treble heat, the thoughtless consequences of which will be likely to break your hearts in future life. Rest assured that the great secret of life is the breathing principle, for which Nature has rightly prepared the material, and the proper mode of using it: and at the incipient stage of life where Mothers are the Physicians, is the easiest place to contract habits against Nature, or to correct them; and that there is woman's post — her appropriate sphere: where she takes to herself the sweetest pleasures of her existence, and draws the highest admiration of the World, whilst, like a guardian Angel, she is watching over, and giving direction to, — the Destinies of Man.

To Children — to Boys and Girls, who have grown up to the age of discretion, and are able to read, the above information and advice are doubly important, because you have long lives of enjoyment or misery before you; and which, you now being out of your Mother's immediate care, are to be controuled by your own actions. And that you may not undervalue the advice which I am about to advance directly to you, I may, (as the Clergyman repeats his text in his Sermon, or a fond parent, the important points of his advice to his son) repeat some things that I have said, while I am giving you further evidence of the importance of the subject I am now explaining to you.

I advise you to bear in mind the awful Bills of Mortality amongst civilized societies, which I have quoted; and realize the dangerous race which civilized man runs in life — how very few —

live to the age designed by Nature — how many perish in infancy, long before they are of your age; and consequently the dangers which you have already passed, and contrast all of these with those of the wild Indians, who by Nature, are no stronger than we are, but who generally live to good old age, with comparatively, few bodily pains in life, and their teeth almost uniformly regular and sound, without the aid of Dentists and tooth-brushes.

Have you observed by those *Bills of Mortality*, that you are but one out of two or three of your little companions who started and commenced playing along with you, permitted to live to boyhood; and also that you have but one chance in four, or thereabouts, of living to tolerable old age?

Can you read those lamentable estimates, which are matters of fact, & draw such fearful conclusions from them as to your own condition and prospects, without realizing the importance of the subject? and can you compare those disasters amongst the civilized, with those of the Savage Races, which I have explained, without believing there is some cause for all this, that is unnatural, and which may be, to a great degree, corrected, if we make the proper effort?

You have read in the foregoing pages, that man's life depends from one moment to another on the air which he breathes, and also that the atmosphere is nowhere pure enough for the healthy use of the lungs until it has passed the purifying process which Nature has prepared in the nostrils, and which has been explained. Air is an Elementary principle, created by the hand of God, who, as has been said, creates nothing but perfections; and consequently is nowhere impure, except from the causes which I have already explained; and in the infinity of His wisdom and goodness, those accidental impurities were foreseen and provided for, even with the brutes, as well as with Mankind) by the mysterious organizations through which the breath of life first came to man.

The various occupations of men, and for which you are by this time preparing, subject them more or less to the dangerous effects of the malaria and poisonous particles in the air, in proportion to the nature of their employments, and the districts and atmospheres in which they exist and work.

The Mechanical trades are the most subject to these, from which the farmer and the Gentleman are more exempt: the Carpenter, therefore, amidst the dust of his shop, should work with his mouth shut, and take care not to sleep upon his bench during his mid-day rest. — the cutlery grinder should not work with his mouth open amidst the particles of steel which his feet raise from the floor, and the motion of his wheel keeps in circulation in the air.

So with the Stone-cutter, (and particularly those working in the hardest sort of stones and flint) the same precautions are necessary; as by the extraordinary proportion of deaths Reported amongst those classes of workmen, the poisonous effects of their business are clearly proved, as well as by the accumulated particles of steel and silex found imbeded in their lungs and coating the Respiratory organs, and which, to have caused premature death, must have been inhaled through the <u>mouth</u>. Physicians are constantly informing the world, in their Reports, of the fatal results of these poisonous things inhaled into the lungs; but why do they not say at the same time, that there are two modes of inhalation, — by the <u>nose</u> and by the <u>mouth</u>; and inform the Mechanics and labourers of the World who are thus risking their lives, that there is safety to life in one way, and great danger in the other? If Physicians forget to give you this advice, these suggestions, with your own discretion, may be of service to you.

The Savages have the advantage of moving about, ...

and sleeping in the open air; and Civlized Races have the advantages over the poor Indians, of comfortable houses and beds, and bed-rooms; and also of the most skilful Physicians and Surgeons, and Dentists; and still we are struck with the deplorable results in our society, of some latent cause of diseases, which I believe has been too much overlooked and neglected.

Have you not many times waked in the middle of the night, in great distress, with your mouths wide open, and so cold and dry that it took you a long time to moisten and shut them again? and did it occur to you at those moments that this was all the result of a careless habit, by which you were drawing an unnatural draught of cold air in every breath, directly on the lungs, instead of drawing it through the nostrils, which Nature has made for that especial purpose, giving it warmth, and measuring its quantity, suitable to the demands of repose?

Watch your little Brothers and Sisters, or other little innocent playfellows, when asleep — with their mouths strained open, and observe the painful expressions of their faces — —

— — their nervous agitation — the unnatural beating of their hearts — the twitching of their — flesh, and the cords of their necks and throats; & your own reason will tell you that they do not enjoy such sleep. —— and on the other hand, what pictures of innocence and enjoyment are those who are quietly sleeping with their mouths firmly shut, and their teeth closed — —— —— ——

—— – —— smiling as they are enjoying their natural repose? If you will for a few moments shut your eyes, and let your under jaw fall down, as it sometimes does in your sleep, you will soon see how painful the over draught of cold air on the lungs becomes, even in the day time, when all your energies are in action to relieve you; and you will instantly perceive the mischief that such a mode of breathing might do in the night, when every muscle and nerve in your body are relaxed, and seeking repose, and the chill of the midnight air is increasing.

It is, most undoubtedly, the above named habit which produces confirmed Snorers, and also consumption of the lungs and many other diseases, as well as premature decay of the teeth — the Nightmare, &c. from which it has been shown, the Savage Races are chiefly exempt; and, (I firmly believe) from the fact that they always sleep with their mouths closed, and their teeth together, as I have before described.

There are many of you who read, to whom this advice will not be necessary, while many others of your little companions will attract your sympathy when you see them asleep, with their mouths strained open, and their sensations — anything but those of joy and rest. Their teeth are growing during those hours, and will grow of unequal lengths, and in unnatural directions, & often times disabling them in after life, from shutting their mouths, even in their waking hours, and most lamentably disfiguring their faces for the remainder of their days.

It is then, my young Readers, for you to evade these evils — to save your own lives and your good-looks, by your own efforts, which I believe the most of you can do, without the aid of Physicians or Dentists, who are always the ready and bold antagonists of disease, but never called until the enemy has made the attack.

I imagine you now just entering upon the stage of life, where you are to come under the gaze of the world, and to make those impressions, and form those connexions in society which are to attend you, and to benefit or to injure you through life. You are just at that period of your existence when the proverb begins to apply, that "man's life is in his own hands"; & if this be not always true, it is quite true, that much of his good looks — his daily enjoyments, and the controul of his habits are within the reach of his attainment. These are all advantages worth striving for, and if you sternly persevere for their accomplishment, you will perfectly verify in your own cases, the other and truer adage, that "at middle age, man is his own best Physician".

I recollect, and never shall forget while I live, that in my boyhood, I fell in love with a charming little girl, merely because her pretty mouth was always shut; her words, which were few, and always (I thought) softly spoken, seemed to issue from the centre of her cherry lips, whilst the corners of her mouth seemed (to me,) to be honeyed together. No excitements could bring more than a sweet smile on her lips, which seemed to hold confident guard over the white and pretty treasures they enclosed, and which were permitted but occasionally, to be seen peeping out.

Of such a mouth it was easy to imagine, even without seeing them, the beautiful embellishments that were within, as well as the sweet and innocent expression of its repose, during the hours of sleep; and from such impressions, I recollect it was exceedingly difficult and painful to wean my boyish affections.

To young people, who have the world before them to choose in, and to be chosen; next to the importance of life itself, and their Future welfare, are the habits which are to disfigure and impair, or to beautify and protect that feature which, with man and with woman, alike, is the most expressive and attractive of the face; and at the same time, the most subject to the influence of pleasing, or disagreeable, or disgusting habits.

Good looks and other personal attractions are desirable, and licenced to all; and much more generally attainable than the world suppose, who take the various features and expressions which they see in the multitude, as the works of Nature's hand.

The natural mouth of man is always an expressive and agreeable feature; but the departures from it, which are caused by the predominance of different passions or tastes, or by the perfectly insipid and disgusting habit which has been explained, are anything but agreeable, and but little in harmony with the advance of his intellect.

Open mouths during the night are sure to produce open mouths during the day; the teeth protrude, if the habit be commenced in infancy, so that the mouth cant be shut — the natural expression is lost — the voice is affected — polypus takes possession of the nose — the teeth decay — tainted breath ensues, and the lungs are destroyed. The whole features of the face are changed —

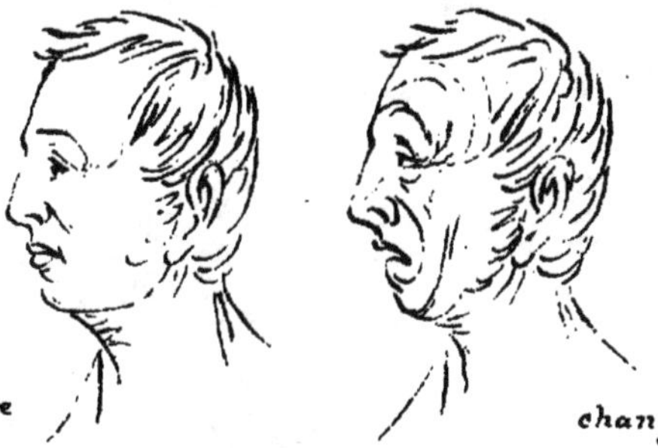

Nature

changed by habit.

— — the under jaw, unhinged, falls and retires — — the cheeks are hollowed, and the cheek-bones and the upper jaw advance, and the brow and the upper eyelids are unnaturally lifted; presenting at once, the leading features and expression of Idiocy.

These are changes in the contour & expression of the face which any one can sufficiently illustrate, with a little effort, on his own face before a looking glass; and that these results are often fixed and permanently retained in society, every sane person is able to discover; and I believe most persons will agree with me, that they are the unfortunate results of the habit I am denouncing.

All the World judge of mens dispositions and character by the expressions of their face; and how disastrous may it therefore be for men to indulge an expression of face in their sleep which they would be ashamed of in their waking hours? The world is full of such, however, — and such a man asleep, and a sleeping Idiot are exactly the same. —— ———

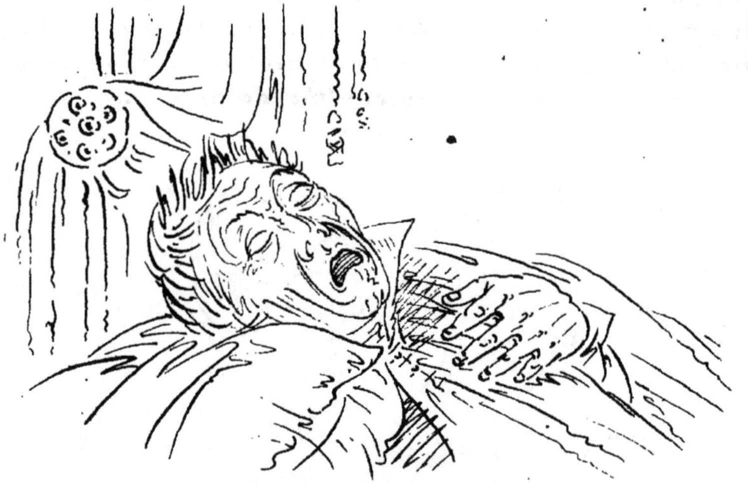

How appalling the thought, and dangerous the habit! and what are likely to be the results shown in the fixed and lasting expressions of the face?

These remarks, & these questions are intended for Boys & Young Men, for I can scarcely allow myself to believe that Young Ladies would be caught sleeping thus. — but one word of advice, even to them, may not be amiss — — Idiots asleep cannot be Angels awake.

The natural mouths of mankind, like those of the brutes, have a general, systematic form and expression; but the various habits and accidents of life give them a vast variety of expressions; and the greater portion of those deviations from Nature, are caused by the malformation of the teeth, or by the falling of the underjaw, which alone, in its intended position forms the natural mouth. When formed in this way, and unchanged by habit or accident, the mouth is always well-shaped and agreeable; but if the teeth become deranged in the manner I have described, the mouth becomes deformed; and in endeavouring to hide that deformity, - oftentimes more disagreeable and unnatural than - when that deformity is exposed.

I knew a young Lady many years ago, amiable and intelligent; and agreeable in every thing excepting the unfortunate derangement and shapes of her teeth; the front ones of which, in the upper jaw, protruding half an inch or more forward of the lower ones, and quite incapable of being covered by the lip, for which there was a constant effort; the result of which was a most pitiable expression of the mouth, and consequently of the whole face, with continual embarrassment and unhappiness of the young Lady, and sympathy of her friends. With all the other charms requisite to have soothed and comforted the life of any man, she lived a life of comparative solitude; and a few years since, - after a lapse of 30. years, I met her again; and though in her old age, she was handsome. — her teeth were all gone, and her lips, from the natural sweetness and serenety of her temper, seemed to have returned to — their native and childish expression, as if making up for the unnatural and painful servitude they had undergone.

The human Mouth, with the great variety of duties it hers to perform, is subject to a sufficient variety of expressions and distortions from abuse, independent of those arising from the habit I am condemning.

The Ear, the Nose, and the Eyes, being less mutable, and less liable to change of character, and shapes, seldom lose their natural expression while original nature is as seldom seen remaining in the expression of the adult mouth.

This feature, from the variety of its — powers and uses, as well as expressions, is undoubtedly the greatest mystery in the material organization of man. In infant Nature it is always innocent and — sweet, and sometimes is even so in adult life.

Its endless modulations of sound may produce the richest, the sweetest of music, or the most frightful and unpleasant sounds in the world. It converses — — it curses, & applauds; — it commends and reproves — it slanders — it flatters — — it prays and it profanes — it blasphemes and adores — blows hot and blows cold — speaks soft tones of love and affection, and rough notes of vengeance and hatred. — it bites, and it woos — it kisses — ejects saliva — eats cherries — Roast Beef, and Chicken, & a thousand other things — — drinks coffee, gin, and — Mint-juleps, (and sometimes Brandy) — takes pills, & Rhubarb and Magnesia — tells tales, and keeps secrets, — is pretty, or is ugly — — of all shapes, and of all sizes — with teeth white — teeth black, and teeth yellow, and with no teeth at all.

During the day, it is generally — eating — drinking — singing — laughing — grinning, pouting — talking — smoking — scolding — whistling —.

— chewing — or spitting — all of which have a tendency to keep it open; and if allowed to be open during the night, is seen, as has been described, by its derangement of the teeth, to create thereby, its own worst deformity.

How strange is the fact, that of the three creations — the Brute — the Savage — and the Civilized Races, the stupid and irrational are taught to perfectly protect and preserve their teeth, through the natural term of life, — the ignorant, Savage Races of mankind, with judgment enough comparatively to do so; when enlightened man, with the greatest amount of knowledge, of pride, and conceit in his good looks, lacks the power to save them from premature decay, and total destruction? showing, that in the enjoyment of his artificial comforts and pleasures, he destroys his teeth, his good looks, and often his life, in his thoughtless departure from natural simplicities and instinct.

The Young Readers, whom I imagine myself now addressing, are old enough to read my advice, & to understand it, and consequently able to make, & to persevere in, their own determined resolutions, — which will be sure to conquer in the end, the habit alluded to, if it has already been allowed to grow upon them.

I advise you to turn back and read again, unless you can distinctly recollect it, the perfect success that I met with in my own case, even at a far more advanced age, and consequently the habit more difficult to correct: and resolve at every moment of your waking hours (except when it is necessary to open them) to keep your lips and teeth firmly pressed together; and your teeth, at all events; under any and every emotion, of pain or of pleasure, of fear — of surprise, or admiration; and from a continual habit of this sort, which will prepare you to meet more calmly and coolly the usual excitements of life, you will find it extending through your sleeping hours, if you will close your lips and your eyes in the fixed determination, and effectually correcting or preventing the disgusting and dangerous habit of sleeping with the mouth open.

Not only manly beauty is produced, and manly firmness of character expressed by a habitual compression of the lips and teeth; but courage — steadiness of the nerves, coolness, and power, are the infallible results.

Men who have been jostled about amongst the vicissitudes of a long life, amidst their fellow men, will have observed that all nervousness commences in the mouth. Men who lack the courage to meet their fellow men in physical combat, are afraid, not of their enemy, nor from a conviction of their own inferiority, but from the disarming nervousness of an open and tremulous mouth, the vibrations of which reach and weaken them, to the ends of their fingers and their toes. In public debates — in the Forum or the Pulpit, a similar alarm results in their certain defeat; and before a hive of Bees, in the same want of confidence, the odour of fear which they emit, is sure to gain them the Sting.

In one of the exciting scenes of my roaming life, I recollect to have witnessed a strong illustration of the above remarks, while residing in one of the Sioux Villages, on the banks of the upper Missouri. A serious quarrel having arisen between one of the Fur Company's men and a Sioux Brave, a challenge was given by the Indian and accepted by the White Man, who were to meet upon the prairie, in a state of nudity, and unattended; and decide the affair with their knives.

A few minutes before this horrible combat was to have commenced, both parties being on the ground, and perfectly prepared, the Factor and myself succeeded in bringing them to a reconciliation, and finally to a shaking of hands, by which we had the satisfaction of know-

-ing, beyond a doubt, that we had been the means of saving the life of one of these men: And a short time afterwards, while alone with the Indian, I asked him if he had not felt fears of his antagonist, who appeared much his superiour in size and in strength — to which he very promptly replied — "no, not in the least; I never fear harm from a man who cant shut his mouth, no matter how large or how strong he may be." I was forcibly struck with this reply, as well as with the conviction I had got in my own mind (and no doubt from the same symptoms) that the white man would have been killed, if they had fought.

That there is an unnatural and lasting contour, as well as an expression of ugliness and lack of manly firmness of character produced in the human face by the habit I have described, every discerning member of society is able easily to decide —

natural. changed by habit.

No one would hesitate a moment in deciding which of these he would have the most reason to fear in battle, or which to choose as his Advocate, for the protection of his life or his property.

No young Lady would delay a moment — in saying which of these, in her estimation, is the best looking young man; or deciding (in her own mind; which of them she would prefer for her Suitor, provided she were to take either.

No one would hesitate in deciding which of these horses to buy. —— (provided the poor Brutes were victims to such misfortunes.)

Nature

habit

And no one, most assuredly, so poor a Physiognomist as not to decide in a moment, which of these young Ladies was the most happy, and which would be likely to get married the first.

and from these innocent and helpless startings in life, it is.

easy to perceive how man's best success, or first and worst misfortunes, are foreshadowed. —— And the fond mother, whilst she watches, in thoughtless happiness, over her sleeping idol, may read in that little open mouth, the certain index to her future sorrows.

It has already been said that man is an "open mouthed animal", and also shown that he is only so by habit, and not by Nature, and that the most striking difference which is found to exist between Mankind in Savage and Civil states, consists in that habit and its consequences, to be found in their relative sanitary conditions.

The American Savage often smiles, but seldom laughs; and he meets most of the emotions of life, however sudden and exciting they may be, with his lips and his teeth closed. He is nevertheless, garrulous and fond of anecdote and jocular fun in his own fire-side cirles; but feels and expresses his pleasure without the explosive action of his muscles, and gesticulation, which characterize the more cultivated Races of his fellow men.

Civilized people, who, from their educations, are more excitable, regard most exciting, amusing, or alarming scenes with the mouth open; as in wonder – astonishment – pain – pleasure, listening, &c. and in laughing, draw pleasure in currents of air through their teeth, by which they insure, (perhaps) pain for themselves, in their sober moments, and for their teeth, diseases and decay which no Dentists can cure.

The Savage, without the change of a muscle of his face listens to the rumbling of the Earthquake, or the thunder's crash, with his hand over his mouth – and if by the extreme of other excitements he is forced to laugh or to cry, his mouth is invariably hidden in the same manner.

As an illustration of some of the above remarks, perhaps "Punch & Judy", which is generally as apt as any other exciting scene to unmask the juveniles, may with effect be alluded to for contrast of expression, as familiar in our streets — — — -- ---

— — — or as it would be viewed (opposite page) by an equal multitude of savage children.

It is one of the misfortunes of Civilization, that it has too many amusing and exciting things for the mouth to say, and too many delicious things for it to taste, to allow of its being closed during the day; the mouth therefore, has too little reserve for the protection of its natural purity of expression; and too much exposure for the protection of its garniture: and, ("good advice is never too late") keep your mouth shut when you read, when you write, — when you listen — when you are in pain — when you are walking — when you are running — when you are riding, and, by all means, when you are angry. There is no person in society but who will find, and acknowledge, improvement in health and enjoyment, from even a temporary attention to this advice.

Mankind, from the causes which have been named, are all, more or less invalids, from infancy to the end of their lives; and he who would make the most of life under these necessary ills; secure his good looks, and prolong his existence; should take care that his lungs and his teeth, however much they may be from habit, or from necessity, abused during the day, should at least be treated with kindness during the night.

The habit against which I am contending, when strongly contracted,

I am fully aware, is a difficult one to correct; but when you think seriously of its importance, you will make your resolutions so strong, and keep them with such fixed and determined perseverance, that you will be sure to succeed in the end.

If you charge your minds during the day sufficiently strong, with any event which is to happen in the middle of the night, you are sure to wake at, or near, the time; and if so, and your minds dwell, with sufficient attention, on the importance of this subject during the day, & you close your eyes and your teeth at the same time, carrying this determination into your sleep, there will be a strong monitor during your rest, that your mouth must be shut; and the benefits you will feel during the following day, from even a partial success, will encourage you to persevere, until, at last, the grand and important object will be accomplished.

One single suggestion more, Young Readers, and you will be ready to be your own Physicians — your own protectors against the horrors of the Night-mare — Snoring, and the dangerous diseases above described.

When you are in a theatre, you will observe that most persons in the pit, looking up to the gallery, will have their mouths wide open; — & those in the gallery, looking down into the pit, will be as sure to have their mouths shut. Then, when you lay your head upon your pillow, advance it a little forward, so as to imagine yourself looking from the Gallery of a Theatre into the Pit, and you have all the secrets, with those beforementioned, for dispelling from you the most abominable and destructive habit that ever attached itself to the human Race.

To Men and Women, of maturer age and

experience, the same advice is tendered; but with them the habit may be more difficult to correct; but with all, it is worth the trial, because there is no possibility of its doing any harm, and it costs nothing.

For the greater portion of the thousands, and tens of thousands of persons suffering with weakness of lungs — with Bronchitis — Asthma - indigestion, and other affections of the Digestive and Respiratory organs, - there is a Panacea in this advice too valuable to be disregarded, and (generally) a relief within their own reach, if they will avail themselves of it.

Approach the bedsides of persons suffering under either of the above dangerous diseases, and they will be found to be sleeping with their mouths wide open, and working their lungs with an over-draught of air upon them, & subject to its midnight changes of temperature as the fires go down; and thus nightly renewing and advancing their diseases which their Physicians are making their daily efforts in vain, to cure.

To such persons my strongest sympathy extends, for I have suffered in the same way: and to them I gladly, and in full confidence of its beneficial results, recommend the the correction of the habit, in the way I have described; their stern perseverance in which will soon afford them relief; and their first night of natural sleep will convince them of the importance of my advice.

Man's life, (in a certain sense) may be said "to be in his own hands" — his body is always closely invested by diseases and death. When awake, he is strong, and able to contend with, and keep out, his enemies; but when he is asleep he is weak: and if the front door of his house be then left open, thieves and robbers are sure to walk in.

There is no harm in my repeating that Mothers should be looked to as the first and principal correctors of this most destructive of human habits; and for the cases which escape their infant cares, or which commence in more advanced stages of life, I have pointed out the way in which every one may be his or her Physician: and the united and simultaneous efforts of the Civilized World should also be exerted in the overthrow of a Monster so destructive to the good looks & life of man. — — — Every Physician should advise his patients, and every Boarding School in existence, and every hospital, should have its surgeon or matron, and every Regiment its Officer, to make their nightly, and hourly, "rounds", to force a stop to so unnatural, disgusting, and dangerous a habit.

Under the working of such a system — mothers guarding and helping the helpless — Schoolmasters their schollars — hospital surgeons their patients, Generals their soldiers, and the rest of the world protecting themselves, a few years would show the glorious results in the Bills of Mortality, and the next generation would be a Re-generation of the Human Race.

The Reader will have discovered, that in the foregoing remarks (unlike the writer of a Play or a Romance, who follows a plan or a plot,) I have aimed only at jotting down, with little arrangement, such facts as I have gained, and observations I have made, in a long and laborious life; on a subject which I have deemed of vast importance to the human Race; and which, from a sense of duty, I am now tendering (in my own hand) to my fellow beings, believing, that if sufficiently read and appreciated, thousands and tens of thousands of the human family may, by their own efforts, rescue their lives, and those of their children, from premature graves.

And in doing this, I take to myself, not only the satisfaction of having performed a positive duty, but the consolations, that what I have proposed can be tried by all classes of society alike, the Rich and the Poor — without pain, without medicine, and without expense. — — and also — that thousands of suffering wanderers in the wildernesses and malaria of foreign lands, as well as of those in the midst of the luxuries of their own comfortable homes, will privately thank me in their own hearts, for hints they will have got from the foregoing pages.

The Proverb, as old and unchangeable as their hills, amongst the N. Amn. Indians — — "My son, if you would be wise, open first your Eyes — your Ears next; and last of all, your Mouth — that your words may be words of wisdom, and give no advantage to thine adversary" — might be adopted with good effect in Civilized life: & he who would strictly adhere to it, would be sure to reap its benefits in his waking hours; and would soon find the habit running into his hours of rest, into which he would calmly enter; dismissing the nervous anxieties of the day, as he firmly closed his teeth and his lips, only to be opened after his eyes and his ears, in the morning; & the rest of such sleep would bear him daily and hourly proof of its value.

And if I were to endeavour to bequeathe to posterity the most important Motto which human language can convey, it should be in three words — —

— — — Shut — your — mouth.

In the social transactions of life, this might have its beneficial results, as the most friendly, cautionary advice, or be received as the grossest of insults; but where I would paint & engrave it — in every Nursery, and on every Bed-post in the Universe, its meaning could not be mistaken; and if obeyed, its importance would soon be realized.

Geo. Catlin.

Appendix.

From the observations, with their results, on board of a Mail Steamer, given in a former page, together with numerous others of a similar nature made whilst I have been in the midst of Yellow fever and the Cholera in the West India Islands and South America; I conscientiously advance my belief — that in any Town or City where either of those pestilences commences its ravages, if that portion of the inhabitants who are in the nightly habit of sleeping with their mouths open were to change their residence to the country, the infection would soon terminate, for want of subjects to exist upon.

This opinion may be startling to many; and if it be combatted, all the better; for in such case the important experiments will more likely be made.

Author.

Rio Grande, Brazil, 1860.

CPSIA information can be obtained
at www.ICGtesting.com
Printed in the USA
LVHW021231280121
677515LV00010B/303

9 780341 752783